Marketing
the
Library

by Benedict A. Leerburger

Knowledge Industry Publications, Inc.

Professional Librarian Series

Marketing the Library

Library of Congress Cataloging in Publication Data

Leerburger, Benedict A.
    Marketing the library.

    (Professional librarian series)
    Bibliography: p.
    Includes index.
    1. Public relations—United States—
Libraries.   I. Title.
Z716.3.L43   021.7'0973   81-18132
ISBN 0-914236-89-X (pbk.)   AACR2

Printed in the United States of America

10   9   8   7   6   5   4   3   2

Table of Contents

List of Tables and Figures

To Ellen, who missed out the first time

Preface

When President John F. Kennedy said, "Books and libraries and the will to use them are among the most important tools our nation has to diffuse knowledge and to develop our powers of creative wisdom,"[1] he summed up a philosophy of librarianship dating back many centuries. The importance of the library as a social institution and the need to support and enhance library services are often ignored by too many individuals. Sadly, these same principles are too often ignored as well by people who should inscribe them in gold—librarians.

The role of the librarian and the library has undergone a significant transformation during the past 20 years. The enormous growth in information, available in both print and non-print form, has been the major force in changing the modern library from a repository of books and manuscripts into a more general information or knowledge-centered facility. In 1963, Yale University professor Derek J. de Solla Price published his treatise *Little Science, Big Science* in which he argued that the growth of information had developed at an empirical and geometric rate. Price stated that there were more scientists alive at that time than the total of all scientists who had previously lived. Further, he argued that the growth of scientific information and scientific publication had occurred at a similar geometric rate. And, according to Price, with the passage of time, information would continue to grow at a pyramiding geometric rate.[2]

Where does this leave the library? As the Librarian of Congress, Daniel J. Boorstin, stated before the White House Conference on Library and Information Services, November 19, 1979:

> The fashionable chronologic myopia of our time tempts enthusiasts to forget the main and proper mission of our libraries. "Libraries have been selling the wrong product for years," one such faddist exclaims. "They have been emphasizing reading. The product that we have is information." But these are false messiahs. Of course, we must use computer technology and enlist the whole information industry. . . . We must never forget that our libraries are our fortresses of knowledge. If we allow these rich

1

resources, still preserved mainly in books, to be displaced by the latest thing, by today's news & journals & preprints & loose-leaf services & telephone conversations & currently revised printouts, we will isolate the world of scholarship from the world of libraries. . . . If librarians cease to be scholars in order to become computer experts, scholars will cease to feel at home in our libraries.[3]

Boorstin makes two key points. To paraphrase the late Marshall McLuhan, the medium must not control the dissemination of the message. Second, for the library to maintain its place in society the patron must "feel at home" in the library. Before the librarian runs out to convert to a totally electronic system in the hope of keeping up with the latest in technology, perhaps it is best to review the role of the library in historical perspective. What is the relation of the library to a free society? Do we still need a library or will the home computer coupled with a massive, central data base serve our requirements?

BRIEF HISTORY OF LIBRARIES

Historically, libraries were created out of need. The ancient Sumerians and Egyptians realized that it was important to maintain custody of a record of the culture to pass down the national heritage from one generation to another. It was also important to store records for training priests, for commerce and for conducting affairs of state. The first public library in the history of Western civilization was probably founded by Peisistratus, the tyrant of Athens, in the sixth century B.C.

By the end of the seventh century, Aristotle had created his Peripatetic School in Athens with a sizable library that became a center of research and study in every field of knowledge of the time. While Aristotle lived, Athens was a world center of learning. Following his death, his library was carted about Asia Minor, ending up in Rome as part of the booty of Sulla, the Roman general and dictator. Thus, several centuries after its creation by Aristotle the great library of Athens became a storehouse of knowledge for Roman scholars.

The greatest library of the ancient world was created by Ptolemy I in Alexandria during the third and fourth centuries B.C. The library was enlarged by Ptolemy II, who may have created the first library acquisition-by-confiscation policy. According to Galen, the illustrious Greek physician of the second century A.D., the library was constantly enlarged by a requirement specifying that all ships entering the harbor give up any manuscripts on board. The great library of Alexandria was destroyed by fire; with it was lost one of the most important collections of materials detailing the ancient world.

During the Middle Ages and the Renaissance, only the wealthy could afford to collect large numbers of books. Many were translations of manuscripts produced by religious orders in Greek or Latin, although the variety and number of books expanded greatly with the invention of moveable type and the growth in literacy during the Renaissance. These private collections provided the core of the important European university and national libraries. The first national library, France's Bibliotheque Nationale, was developed from the private collections of French kings Charles V, Charles VI, Charles VIII and Louis XI. King Francis I brought the collection together at the palace of Fountainbleau and named the first librarian, Guillaume Budé, to oversee the material. The Bodleian Library in England and the Biblioteca Medicea-Laurentiana Library in Italy soon followed as important libraries making available collections of manuscripts to scholars.

LIBRARIES IN THE U.S.

In the United States, libraries started in a similar fashion with small, private collections being incorporated into larger collections, primarily for use by scholars. In 1638 Rev. John Harvard left his personal library of some 300 volumes to the new college in Cambridge, MA. By the end of the 17th century the College of William and Mary also had its own library and by the middle of the 18th century Yale University also had a considerable collection.

In 1656 a Boston merchant, Robert Keayne, established a library that was open to the public. Although it was a small collection by today's standards, it was a most important addition to the Boston scene. His library served the community for several generations. The concept of a subscription library is credited to Benjamin Franklin when, in 1731, he and other Philadelphia citizens contributed to a book collection that would circulate freely among themselves. Franklin's Library Company of Philadelphia was the forerunner of other subscription libraries that bloomed throughout the country. Rhode Island's Redwood Library in Newport and South Carolina's Charleston Library Society still exist today.

The free public library supported by public monies was not started until long after the birth of subscription libraries. In 1833, Peterborough, NH established the first tax-supported library. Within a few years a number of state and city governments in Massachusetts, Maine and New Hampshire followed suit. Other communities realized that public funding for libraries was an important element in developing a strong local educational/cultural base. By 1875 there were 2000 free libraries owning more than 1000 books each; by 1900 the free libraries numbered 5400.

The growth of the free library system in America received a significant boost around the turn of the century when Andrew Carnegie, the Scottish-born industrialist and steel magnate, contributed millions of dollars to the building of libraries on the condition that the individual towns and cities receiving grants establish and properly finance the libraries by taxes.

The number of public libraries in the United States today is unknown. More than 8300 community library *systems* existed in 1980, with countless separate branches. In the non-public sector, there were as of 1976 an estimated 3000 academic libraries and 5287 special libraries, in addition to the three national libraries (Library of Congress, National Library of Medicine, National Agricultural Library). Together they house more than 1 billion volumes.[4]

To these figures must be added the millions of periodicals in library collections and the "newer" information resources: microforms, phonograph records, audio and video cassettes, and electronic information retrieval services that many believe are revolutionizing the nature of the library. With the use of computers and online retrieval services, the library's collection is no longer confined to the materials within its walls. And the availability of information, sometimes only minutes old, is but a few keystrokes away.

THE LIBRARY AND SOCIETY

But the library is more than the sum of its materials, whether inside or outside the building itself. It is more than a link in the communications system. It is an essential element in the growth and development of society. In marketing the library, we are selling a growing communications network that has answers to questions ranging from science and technology to business and the humanities. Libraries have become job information centers, lecture halls, art galleries, public meeting rooms, theaters and much more. No other social organ meets such a multiplicity of needs.

In the largest sense, when we market the library we are marketing ideas and the free flow of information to all segments of the community. We are marketing our cultural and intellectual heritage. We are preserving a bastion of a literate, informed and free society.

With growing financial pressures on the library, decisions must be made which will affect the relationship between the library and the community it serves. Many libraries are reducing hours of service, trimming staff, limiting acquisitions. Others are considering the imposition of fees for special services such as data base searching or for out-of-town users. The imposition of fees would seem to betray the whole ideal of free access to information that libraries are meant to promote.

However, purists who insist that the library must never bend to the winds of increased costs must also ask the question: How can a library continue to provide special services to a few patrons without compromising the general services to all patrons? A patron who requests an online bibliographic search, for example, is using the facilities of the public library for a special, but certainly valid purpose. The whole *raison d'être* of the library is to serve its community and provide information. The fact that the library may well incur a cost ranging from $6 to more than $30 for the search should not be the concern of the patron wanting answers. However, if every patron requested the same service the library would be out of business within a week. Where does the library draw the line?

An analysis of the issues involved in charging fees for library services is beyond the scope of this book. But the fact that this question is being raised throughout the information world points up the growing need of libraries to ensure and increase community support. To do so, the library must get its message to the public. Effective marketing techniques will help the library to do just that. It is hoped that this book will provide the means to that end.

FOOTNOTES

1. *The Public Papers of the Presidents of the United States, 1961-1963.* (Washington, DC: U.S. Government Printing Office, 1964).

2. Derek J. de Solla Price, *Little Science, Big Science* (New York: Columbia University Press, 1963).

3. Daniel J. Boorstin, *Gresham's Law: Knowledge or Information?* (Washington, DC: Library of Congress, 1980), p. 4.

4. Robert Wedgeworth, ed., *ALA World Encyclopedia of Library and Information Services* (Chicago, IL: American Library Association, 1980), p. 580.

1

Marketing: A Response to a Need

Telling a librarian to prepare for hard times is like telling consumers that prices are going up. Budget cuts, along with increased prices for books, periodicals and general services, have become so commonplace in today's library that reminders are unnecessary. These increased costs and funding cutbacks have affected large and small libraries across the nation.

In our nation's capital, bookmobile service, once a key ingredient in bringing books to the city's low income population, has been curtailed. The total number of library employees has been cut by close to a third; employees working in the branch libraries have seen their hours cut by more than 40%. One of the nation's largest library systems, the Los Angeles County Public Library, went for more than a year without buying a new book. The New York Public Library system has more than 200,000 books in storage awaiting the service of catalogers. In Boston, Mayor Kevin White announced that the city's 1980-81 budget would be cut by 10% across the board; this meant a library budget reduction of $1 million. The Boston Public Library requested funds for 581 positions but only received enough for 480.

In Colorado, a request to increase the Denver Public Library's budget for 1982 by 5.1% was denied, and funding was frozen at the 1981 level. Library director Henry Shearouse announced that the library would cope by eliminating 23 staff positions and reducing branch hours by 50%. In addition, the library announced the imposition of substantial fees for non-residents: $200 per year for a family, $100 for an individual and $10 a day for a user without an annual permit. Most of the Denver Public Library's financial bind is the result of cutbacks in state funds.

The story is similar in Oregon. The Oregon State Library reported a 15% reduction—more than $317,000—in the State Library's general fund as a result of action by the legislature. How did this cut affect the people of Oregon? Aside from eliminating six full-time library positions, the state reduced book budgets by $22,000, books for institutions by $20,000, per capita aid to local communities by $75,000 and establishment grants by $24,000.

From state to state, the literature becomes repetitious. With combined recession and inflation it seems that the library is caught in the middle. Of course there is no easy answer to the problem. However, Snow F. Grigsby, a Detroit public relations research consultant and, at 82 years of age, the oldest delegate to the 1979 White House Conference on Library and Information Services, perhaps provided a partial solution when he said:

> Detroit, which prides itself on its "Renaissance" image, and the Detroit Board of Education sat by and watched the closing of 63 libraries throughout the city. Could we refer to this act of ignorance as "urban decay" or "potential brain waste"?
> I would suggest that we pursue a radical change of image for the library. We must establish some kind of public relations department to sell the community on the importance of the library in the neighborhood as well as the school. We should emulate the leadership of our major labor unions, with strong and forceful lobbying in our state and national capitals. After all, our library personnel and our organizations have been silent for too long, thus having suffered major cuts in funding.[1]

THE ROLE OF MARKETING

Grigsby sums up both the problem and a direction toward a solution when he suggests that *public relations* is an essential ingredient in the operation of today's library system. In the past the idea of a librarian "selling" anything was tantamount to suggesting that the public library also act as a local employment agency. Yet the modern library is doing just that: assisting job hunters to find work. The modern library has also recognized that marketing may well be as important to its future as the ability to catalog a book or manage the reference desk. In an address before the spring 1979 conference of the Missouri Association of College and Reference Libraries, Joyce A. Edinger of the University of Missouri-St. Louis Library talked about marketing the library.

> Marketing is an activity that for years has been used successfully within the profit sector of the economy to promote demand for products and services. Recently, however, nonprofit organizations—including libraries—have come to realize that marketing activities are related and relevant to the management of their operations also. The obvious reason for librarians to become involved in a formalized effort of this nature is to improve the satisfaction of the potential library patron.[2]

Public relations, or to use the more contemporary phrase, *marketing,* is certainly not a new concept. When the first librarian put the first "silence" sign in the library, an attempt was made to influence the public's attitude. A simple but realistic definition of marketing is suggested by Philip Kotler in *Marketing for Nonprofit Organizations*: "Marketing refers to the effective management by an organization of its exchange relations with its various publics."[3]

The Effect of Successful Marketing

The influence of a successful library marketing campaign can be demonstrated almost daily. Previously we mentioned the cutback of services in the District of Columbia. In the summer of 1980 an additional $2.9 million cutback was proposed by the mayor. A strong marketing effort on behalf of the library was initiated by the system. According to Hardy

Franklin of the Public Library of the District of Columbia, "Both *The Washington Post* and *Star* came out against the cut, and with strong media and citizen support we had restored $1.5 million of the funds and were consequently able to keep all our libraries open on a reduced schedule . . . the mayor is still getting letters opposing library budget cuts. . . ."[4]

Although the 1980 elections saw the citizens of many states vote down increases in state funding, much of it designated for libraries, there were some positive results. In all cases in which the public stood behind the library and rejected cuts in funding, there was evidence of a successful marketing effort on behalf of the library. One case in point is the Harford County Library in Bel Air, MD.

In 1978 a tax revolt in Bel Air was successful when Proposition 62 was supported by a two-to-one margin, carrying every precinct. In 1980 another effort was made to cut taxes. Local Question J would have set taxes back to 1978 levels. Needless to say, passage of this proposal would have had a direct effect on every library. According to Ruby Starr, publicity coordinator for the Harford County Library, "The cutback in funding could have been as high as 30%, although there's no way of telling exactly how the losses would be split."[5] The library would have had to cancel plans for two new branches, and eliminate programs like preschool outreach and all other "nonessential" services. Harford aligned itself "with unions, management, community organizations, newspapers and politicians" in opposing this threat. The alliance, through an active public relations effort designed to benefit all groups, sought to let the public know exactly what services they would lose should the second tax rollback be endorsed. The public not only got the message but responded at the polling booth. Unlike Proposition 62 which sailed through, Question J was defeated.

There are other success stories. New York libraries gained a $7.5 million increase in state aid for 1981-82, the largest increase ever voted for libraries. Much credit for this achievement went to the efforts of thousands of librarians, trustees and patrons who exhorted their state representatives to support library needs. Similarly, in Pennsylvania a massive volunteer effort helped bring about an appropriations increase of $3.2 million in 1981, a per capita increase of nearly 33%. And in Columbus, OH, voters renewed a tax levy providing the Public Library of Columbus & Franklin County with one third of its revenue. As Rich Sweeney, the library's director, put it: "We went to the people and they came out and voted for us."[6]

Commitment to the Marketing Concept

The need to assure adequate funding is only one element in a library marketing effort. The overriding goal of marketing is to assure that the library will remain in the forefront as an information center within the community. An effective program is a cooperative effort. In many cases, it requires reorienting each staff member's relationship to those who rely on the library's services: the patrons. The patron, or client, becomes the focus of the library; he or she is the librarian's reason for being.

A successful marketing program requires commitment from every staff member to what has been called the "marketing concept." According to Kotler, "The marketing concept requires integrated marketing; the various departments in the organization must realize that the actions they take have a significant effect on the organization's ability to create, retain and satisfy consumers.''[7] After the marketing concept has been accepted by the library staff— and "selling" the concept may well involve a solid marketing effort by the director or board of trustees—it is important to evaluate the strengths and weaknesses of the library's current programs and policies. The director then should define the goals of the marketing program. The next step is to plan a course of action that achieves these goals.

DEVELOPING A MARKETING PLAN

Since each library has its own criteria based on the needs and characteristics of its clients, it is important to review the population, or marketplace, served by the library. Who currently uses library services? What are the future needs of the community? For example, if there is a large senior citizens' population in the area, does the library have information about agencies available to serve the elderly? If the community has a major industrial facility, does the library serve the workers by providing job-related information and management by providing current economic and other business data? Is there a good collection of children's books in a community with a high percentage of young families?

The second stage in developing a marketing plan should focus on the specific methods the library can use to increase community awareness of current and future services. What can be done to make it easier for the client to gain access to the collection? How can the wealth of information contained in the library be spread throughout the community? What can the library do to inform the marketplace that the information exists?

A marketing plan's final phase coordinates the needs of the library with its financial and personnel resources. A full page ad in the local newspaper may attract the community's attention to the library's message; however, the cost-effectiveness of such an ad might be questionable. On the other hand, an article in the local newspaper about a new service, recently received books or forthcoming lecture costs the library nothing and is probably more effective.

MARKETING METHODS

Basically, there are three major means of marketing available to the library: the published word, personal contact and what architects and designers call "atmospherics."

The Published Word

The published word refers to that wide blend of activities ranging from an article in the local or college paper to an announcement on television. Librarians have been sending out the written message for years. Posters, newsletters, reports, press releases and bibliographies on specific subjects are all common and excellent methods of "spreading the word." That old-fashioned "silence" sign has given way to signs pointing to record rooms, microform reading rooms and public meeting rooms where talking is encouraged. The use of nonprint media—broadcast and cable television, as well as radio—is increasing. The published word is one way the librarian tells the community: here is what we can do for you.

Personal Communication

Although the published word is the most common means of marketing library services, personal contact can be equally effective. Colleges and universities offer particularly fertile ground for this method.

Librarians should seek contact with faculty and administrators to discuss available and needed library services. At some schools, a librarian serves as a liaison with academic departments to assist faculty members in information gathering or problem solving. Through such personal contact, librarians can keep abreast of new developments—e.g., new courses, directions in research and potential problem areas—that may involve the library.

Now that computers and data base searching have become integral features at academic and larger public libraries, there is a growing need to work more directly with patrons to educate them in the use of these newer services. In return, librarians find that direct communication gives them a better understanding of the needs and problems that users and potential users may have.

The public librarian should also be aware of activities within the local schools and community organizations. Contact through a liaison with school librarians or school-student library committees can be most effective. Some librarians have established direct contact with local colleges and schools offering adult education programs; librarians are often called upon to teach courses or assist in providing backup material for ongoing courses. Through contact with community groups, the library can become an essential ingredient in many groups' planning. A personable, knowledgeable librarian can be a library's strongest asset in any public relations effort.

It is important to develop and maintain an ongoing relationship with the power structure within the community. The establishment of library support groups such as a Friends of the Library can be an important element in selling the library's needs to a community.

Atmospherics

The term "atmospherics" refers to the concept of designing the library building with consideration for the people who use it. It also implies concern for the patron's comfort, psychologically, as well as physically. Staff attitude is crucial. The building must exude a welcoming feeling. To enter a building that looks forbidding, to be greeted by an unsmiling face or an attitude that the patron is somehow intruding, will result in disaster. The library must be a pleasant place where people will enjoy spending time. Or, at least not mind spending time. If the layout is so imposing that it is hard to find a book or even an individual who can provide assistance, patrons are not going to spend any more time in the building than they absolutely have to.

STRUCTURE OF THIS BOOK

The purpose of this book is not to sell the concept of public relations to librarians. Rather, it is to explore and define specific ways in which libraries are currently "selling" their services. By providing librarians with a basic guide to do-it-yourself marketing, it is hoped that the message can be spread with minimum cost, maximum efficiency and some pleasure en route. The avenues of communicating with a community are vast and varied. Librarians must learn how to use them effectively.

Chapter 2 will discuss basic publicity techniques, particularly use of the media. Chapter 3 describes special programs and events that libraries can offer as a means of attracting community support. Developing community relations, including the formation of Friends of the Library groups, is the subject of Chapter 4. Marketing efforts related specifically to fund raising will be described in Chapter 5. Although this book concentrates on marketing for public libraries, it will not ignore academic or other special libraries. Chapter 6 provides information on marketing techniques for nonpublic libraries.

In basic ways, however, the marketing needs of all libraries are similar and methods may be identical. For the survival of any library it is essential to "sell a need." It is essential for the library to work closely with its supporting community—whether town, university or corporation—and to be constantly aware of that community's needs. It is essential to respond to those needs—and to make sure that the community *knows* that the library *is* responding to them. Only then will the library flourish.

FOOTNOTES

1. Snow F. Grigsby, as quoted in a 1979 White House Conference press release.

2. Joyce A. Edinger, "Marketing Library Services: Strategy for Survival," *College & Research Libraries* (July 1980): 328.

3. Philip Kotler, *Marketing for Nonprofit Organizations* (Englewood Cliffs, NJ: Prentice-Hall, 1975).

4. *Library Journal* 105 (December 15, 1980): 2532.

5. Ibid.

6. *Library Journal* 106 (August 1981): 1474.

7. Kotler, op. cit.

2

Basic Publicity Techniques

There are probably as many varieties of public libraries as there are villages, towns and cities. Each library must consider itself unique; each serves a specific type of patron. However, all libraries, regardless of size or clientele, have common bonds. All are concerned with their relevance in the community and must fulfill their purpose as information centers. Many also serve as centers of recreation. All libraries must concentrate their efforts on a single key element: *service*. Without it there is no need to market the library.

The variety of services a library has to offer must be known to as many people in the community as possible. Edward J. Montana Jr., of the Boston Public Library, put it this way: "Keeping the library in the public's mind continually by fostering community relations and a steady build-up of goodwill among the various elements of a community by telling the 'library's story,' to use a hackneyed phrase, will do much to ensure not only its widespread use but also widespread support when it is needed."[1]

WHO HANDLES PUBLIC RELATIONS?

It is generally agreed that one staff member should be assigned the overall responsibility for public relations. In most smaller libraries, the individual chosen knows little about the specialty but has the desire to learn. For the larger public library, particularly in urban areas, a professional public relations specialist should be seriously considered. The PR manager should have an understanding of the workings of the system but does not need a degree in library science. Remember, he or she must wear two hats: as the public's representative on the library staff and as the library's representative to the public.

The basic qualities required of the public relations specialist are the same whether the individual is an outside professional or a staff member. Selling in all forms is a people-related activity; the PR specialist must like people and have the ability to get along with them. Meeting a deadline, dealing with printers and mailers, listening to an irate patron who "deposited the book in the book drop last week despite what they say at the circulation desk" can be harrowing. The job is not for a lover of the tranquil.

Of course, the public relations individual should be sincere and able to stick with an assignment even if it becomes unpleasant. The ability to write well, quickly and on schedule is important. There are many intangibles that separate a good PR person from an ordinary one: the ability to recognize a story, to "sell" news of the library to the media, to know that a forthcoming library event will catch the public's attention, to identify a potential problem before it becomes a public nuisance. The PR person should have a wide variety of interests and be able to accept new ideas and radical solutions.

Previous experience in journalism, publishing or the social services is a real plus. In many communities a volunteer with previous public relations experience can be found through an ad in the local newspaper. An experienced volunteer has the advantage over a staff member assigned to the task because the volunteer is usually able to devote time *solely* to the public relations function; the individual, if properly selected, knows the ways of the community; and, best of all, the price is right.

THE LOCAL NEWSPAPER

To keep the community aware of library activities and policies, the PR individual must take advantage of the local organs for information dissemination. Perhaps no single source can provide such widespread coverage of library events, news and policy changes as the local newspaper.

In large cities, the so-called local paper is primarily national in scope and finds it easy to relegate library releases to the back pages or the trash can. However, even in major metropolitan centers, there are many local newspapers aimed at a select audience. They may be neighborhood papers, foreign-language papers, or special-interest papers with an emphasis on food, real estate, etc. Each of these local papers reaches members of your library community, but rarely are these publications considered a viable means of selling the library. However, a creative public relations individual can use them effectively. A Spanish-language paper, for example, might be interested in stories about the library's collection of materials in Spanish or on Hispanic subjects. Columns devoted to reviews of new books, travel information or exhibits with a particular ethnic angle are welcomed by editors eager to serve their special audiences.

Making the Initial Contact

Most small circulation newspapers rely heavily on the editor in chief for suggesting story ideas and managing the newsgathering activities. The editor is easily accessible and eager for new ideas. Better yet, if you can provide a complete story that needs only minor editing, you have saved the editor's time. It is most important to meet the editor and cultivate an ongoing relationship. Often you may discover that the editor has assigned a cultural affairs editor or community news editor to monitor the library along with a shopping list of other potential news areas within the community.

The initial contact with the editor will enable you to identify the person responsible for library coverage and set up a meeting. A joint meeting with both the editor and the reporter covering the library can provide an even stronger liaison. There are a few simple "do's" and "don'ts" that should be observed during this first meeting.

• Do come prepared with specific suggestions. These may be ideas for periodic columns such as a book review column, children's reading list, activities column, etc.

• Don't ask the editor what he or she may like in the way of library coverage. If the editor had library stories in mind you would have heard about it. Remember your job is to sell, not shop.

• Do learn as much as you can about the newspaper and its audience before you meet the editor. You don't want to suggest subjects that might be taboo to a newspaper's special audience. On the other hand, by knowing the paper's typical reader you are in a much stronger position to suggest a weekly column geared to the interests of that audience.

• Don't assume that the library is going to provide the paper with front page news. You represent a service organization. The product you have to sell is service.

• Do ask the editor how you may submit written copy to make the editor's job simpler. Although there is a standard way to write a news story or press release, some editors prefer copy typed to fit certain specifications.

• Don't assume that all editors believe in the First Amendment and will rush to fly the banner of controversy. Your library's recent lecture on sex education in the schools might be of major interest to you, but the paper may not want the story if it feels the subject is too hot to handle.

Preparing a Press Release

The basic way to submit material to the newspaper is through a written press release. It is possible that your local editor or reporter is willing to take a story over the phone; however, there are potential problems in this method. Too often facts are garbled. And the slant that you would like the story to take is often lost. It is better to submit a formal release, and then allow the editor to get back to you with any unanswered questions or problems. A sample press release is shown in Figure 2.1.

The press release need not be a formal document but it should follow some simple, basic guidelines. Here are a few of the basics:

• Type all your communications. You are a professional organization and all material coming from your library should have a professional appearance.

• The name of the issuing body should appear on your press release. This may simply

Figure 2.1   The Press Release

You don't need special press release paper. This is enough.

From: The Administrative Offices
      Baltimore County Public Library
      320 York Road
      Towson, Maryland 21204

Essential. Editor looks at this first.

For Release: Monday a.m. Papers, February 13, 1978

Story in a nutshell. Useful for headline writing.

APPLICATIONS FOR SENIOR CITIZEN DISCOUNTS

The essentials of the story. Can be used as a spot as is on the radio.

Applications for senior citizen discounts cards, issued by the Baltimore

County Commission on Aging, are now available at all 18 branches of the Baltimore

County Public Library.

when this happens, don't worry.

Eligible for the cards are all (ciitzens) of Baltimore County sixty years

of age and over. The applications can be filled out at the library, which will

forward them to the Commission on Aging, or they can be mailed by the applicant to

the Commission. Application forms may also be taken by family members and friends to

give to older citizens.

Keep paragraphs short.

A Directory of Aging Services in Baltimore County, which has been developed

by the Baltimore County Commission on Aging, is also available in limited quantities

at branches of the Baltimore County Public Library.

An "add on" story related to the first part of the release.

This directory lists the services and programs available to older adults in

the County, including discounts, education, employment, financial aid, health,

housing, legal, nutrition, recreation and volunteer organizations, social services

and home care, telephone reassurance and transportation.

The directory is available, while quantities last, free of charge. In the

event that free copies for distribution have been exhausted, library patrons can see

the branch library copy, which is retained at the branch for reference.

# # #

Essential -- in case of questions.

For Further Information Call:
Geoffrey W. Fielding
Special Projects Officer
Telephone: 296-8500

Double space all releases. Triple space between paragraphs 50 "breaklines" can be written in Use one side of sheet only.

Source: Baltimore County Public Library. Reproduced with permission.

be the library's name and address, but it might also be a committee or subcommittee working within the library.

• Also provide the name of an individual who can supply additional information, and be sure to include a telephone number. Some organizations provide both the library number and the individual's home number. The concept being conveyed is that you're giving the paper a news story that has a sense of immediacy. If the editor has a need to reach you quickly, you're available. The individual's title or area of responsibility should also be stated on the release.

• The subject or lead is usually typed in capital letters and centered across the top of the release. This brief heading provides the essence of the story and also gives the editor a basis for composing the actual headline that will appear in the paper.

• Include a release date. There is rarely a need to release a library story at a specific time. However, since you may be sending your release to both weekly and daily papers it is better to date your release to conform to the needs of the weekly paper. If it doesn't matter, simply state, "For Immediate Release." The problem you can encounter is that the weekly paper, knowing it will be beaten by the daily, will ignore your story.

• A coded reference number is sometimes useful. Although smaller libraries do not have the problem of filing and recording releases, many PR organizations will code the date or internal number of the release. This code usually appears on the last page of the release in the lower right hand corner. (For example, July 14, 1982 would appear as 071482.)

• Use only one side of the page. Special paper isn't necessary; however, some libraries do use printed or mimeographed sheets with the library's name or logo on the sheet. The advantage of this is primarily one of identification. The newspapers that receive your releases know immediately that you have a message for them. Larger papers in urban areas receive so many press releases each day that a means of immediate identification is most helpful for the editors.

• Double space all press releases and leave a triple space between paragraphs.

• The first paragraph of your press release should contain all the elements of your story. Remember the basics of journalism: who, what, when, where. Your first paragraph should be structured to stand alone. (It can also be sent to the local radio station and can be used as a spot news announcement without rewriting.)

• Tell your story completely, but don't embellish it. Editors are used to "pap." They see it every day. The library doesn't have to prepare a feature article under the guise of a press release. Although some editors claim that they would rather see more than less in a release, don't include more information than is really necessary.

• Either photocopy or multilith your press releases. Don't use carbon paper or send an original to one paper and a copy to another. You can count on the second paper finding out that its competitor received the original. You need friends, not enemies.

• Maintain a consistent style. Paragraphs should not be divided from one page to the next unless absolutely unavoidable. Number all pages, and use the word "more" at the bottom of a page if the copy continues. Leave generous margins. Choose a standard style book (e.g., *A Manual of Style,* published by the University of Chicago Press) and stick to it.

• Have someone else proofread your press release. Writers are not effective proofreaders of their own copy.

What Is News?

The subject of your press releases should vary as the services and activities of the library vary. Basically, your release must do two things: educate and inform. If there is to be an event (for example, a speaker) at the library, the release should provide all pertinent information. In addition to the basic "who, what, when, where," it should offer information to stimulate interest in the subject of the talk. As a librarian, there is no one better to do research on a subject than you. Do your work thoroughly. Include some interesting details. Of course, a description of the speaker is a must. If the individual is listed in one of the standard reference works, your job is much simpler. Don't be afraid to write or call the speaker and request biographical information for the press. If the library has a few basic books on the speaker's subject, these can be mentioned at the end of your release.

Write your release with the assumption that the reader knows little about the subject. Don't write down, but don't assume the reader is an expert. Informing or educating the public about new library features can be particularly difficult—and important—as electronic technology in libraries becomes more prevalent. An educational program can be developed initially through a series of press releases announcing the new system, describing its advantages and possible difficulties, and explaining how it will benefit library users. Follow-up releases, displays and seminars in the library are well worth considering. (More information on special programs will be given in Chapter 3.)

The question of "what is news?" is a valid one in promoting library services. From the library's point of view, news is simply information not known to the general public. Interpreting the news or evaluating an event to determine whether or not it is newsworthy is another matter. The acquisition of a new book may be a "news event" but certainly not worthy of a press release. However, the acquisition of a major work is well worth a press release. For example, if your reference department has just received the 1980 edition of the 20-volume *New Grove Dictionary of Music and Musicians,* a release stating only that the book is now in the library probably will never see print. However, a description of the massive work's history, scope and value to the community could make an interesting news or feature story.

Many local papers are interested in publishing a library column (see Figure 2.2). This column can be devoted to a review of a major book, a listing of important acquisitions, a roundup of recent library events and planned future activities or, for the weekly paper, a box, "What's Happening at the Library," in which future programs are listed.

Figure 2.2   Clippings from *The Cairo Messenger* Weekly Library Column

THE CAIRO MESSENGER, FRIDAY APRIL 10, 1981

TWO—C

LIBRARY SPECIAL

The problems of teenagers will again be spotlighted Tuesday afternoon, April 7th at 4 p.m., with the preview of the film ALMOST A MAN, the story written by Richard Wright. This is a part of a planned series on alienation as reflected in suicide, ranking second in deaths among teenagers in the United States.

ALMOST A MAN deals with a runaway and in a sensitive manner reflects on youth confronting the estrangement between parent and child. A discussion will follow. Parents, counselors, ministers, and neighbors are invited for this.

This film will not interfere with the beginning short story series to be held at 7:30 p.m.

YOUR PUBLIC LIBRARY IS YOURS

USE IT

Spring has arrived with all the splash of colors that we ̶e come to appreciate after bleakness of winter. As l, heralding the birth of a vernal season, the birds t in force.

seemingly, the Library atrons are out in force. the most often questions of late around identifying

 ̶mong the most creatures, birds ̶ed and inspired ̶̶ since the beginning of time. Poems and songs have been written to their grace and the freedom thev symbolize.

We are not di ̶̶ is

̶p by the Public Library ̶ext time you appreciate the wonder of a bird and read about them. Your appreciation will grow. The following list is a small portion of the Roddenbery Memorial Library's collection on birds:

The Book of Bird Life - Allen
Audubon Society Field Guide to North American Birds: Eastern Division
Joys of a Garden for Your Birds - Barrington
Thoreau on Birds - Cruickshank
American Song Birds - Eden
Treasury of Birdlovers - Krutch
How to Attract, House and Feed Birds - Schulz
Flashing Winds - Terres
Birdcraft - Wright
 ̶eorgia **Birds** - Burleigh
Birds of Grady County - ̶ddard
 ̶ure **Society News** (Per- ̶l)

I remember the Rodden- ̶emorial Library is one ̶est places around for ̶̶ birds.

̶ Public Library is

Library Film-Dis̶ Is Schedu̶

"The Blue Hote̶ scheduled second film ̶ ion sponsored by the library to be held Tuesday night, April 14th, at 7:30

This story written by Stephen Crane concerns three men given shelter in a small Nebraska town about 1880.

̶gnights Crane's imagination. His van Gogh and ̶ Film evokes the ̶ development of their s. It offers a slice out

̶comed by the library.

A small donation

Badge of Courage" (1895) Crane's novel "The Red became a best seller and catapulted the young writer to fame.

The planned films-discussion held weekly on Tuesday evenings at 7:30 at the libr ̶ will end on May 5th.

QUESTION OF THE WEEK

QUESTION:
What is the fastest flying

FIVE—C

 ̶ over due to do is go leave the ̶s and get a coupon for ̶ free ice cream cone.

McDonalds will bring your books back to the library in Cairo - fair enough? Now this is a special time - because beginning Sunday April 5th is National Library Week, lasting through Saturday, April 11th.

McDonalds at Highway 84 in Cairo, your library friend and your friend.

Bring those overdue books back. Only one week for this offer. A fair exchange. Overdue books for a coupon for a free ice cream cone. ̶onalds has done it again!

̶e overdue Books ̶o McDonalds And Get Free Ice Cream

McDonalds, those public spirited folk, want you to read, they also want you to return the books that you borrow from your Public Library in Cairo.

̶w they are going to help

THE CAIRO MESSENGER, FRIDAY APRIL 10, 1981

A follow-up release describing a lecture or concert that has already occurred may well be worthy of a news item. A portable tape recorder is an excellent way to preserve a speaker's words. Permission to record a speaker should be obtained in advance and, wherever possible, direct quotes should be checked with the speaker before submitting them to the press.

Photographs

Photographs are also welcomed by local papers. Most newspapers require black-and-white glossies and do not accept color photographs. Although some papers will accept Polaroids, reproduction quality is better if 8-inch by 10-inch non-Polaroids are submitted. The size can be smaller but it is better to check with your local editor before submitting pictures. Often, the paper will assign a staff photographer to cover a specific assignment if the subject matter warrants it. Again, when selling your story it doesn't hurt to sell the idea that the story can be improved with pictures. You must, however, exercise some judgment. Don't try to heavily promote a story that isn't worth it. Your credibility with editors is very important. Protect it!

A legal point should be raised in conjunction with the use of photographs. If you ask a subject to pose, or film an individual in action, have the person or persons sign a "no payment rights" form to protect the library from a commercial rights claim. The form should make it clear that your subject has no objection to being photographed and allows the library to use the photograph in any and all ways the library chooses. Another legal consideration is the use of existing photographs, art work or video tapes that may be in the library's collection. Although the library may own the actual material, it may not own the rights to reproduce the work. A call to the town's legal officer or to a local attorney should give you a quick answer.

CONSIDER THE AIR WAVES

The printed page is only one way to spread your message. The local radio and TV stations can be extremely valuable assets in your marketing campaign. With the rapidly growing acceptance of cable television, the opportunities for libraries to take advantage of air time is better than ever.

In evaluating the best media for your library's marketing effort, it is important to place your news item or public service message in proper perspective. The announcement of a coming book fair could be covered in the spot news segment or as a public service announcement by your local radio station, but might not warrant consideration on television. The actual event, however, could make an interesting television spot. Thus, planning is an important element in deciding on the proper media for coverage and in designing the message itself. Broadcasting, like print journalism, offers several avenues of approach: the basic news story, public service announcement, longer broadcast "specials" devoted to a specific subject or format, and the visual story.

The major difference between broadcast news and print journalism is the depth of coverage. While print people usually include details in their reportage, the person behind the microphone has time only for the highlights of the story. Newsworthiness is the key when submitting a release to the broadcaster. The news release you send your local paper probably will not do. It should be shorter, more to the point and, if possible, written for a newscaster to use as a script.

The Public Service Announcement

For information concerning the library, the public service announcement is most appropriate. This brief message, designed to fit into a 15-60 second slot on radio or TV, can alert members of the community to an event, service or activity being planned by the library. The public service release is not a news story, a paid ad or an ongoing broadcast. It is simply a message that the local station may use at its discretion at various times during the broadcast day or week. (See Figure 2.3.)

Usually, the decision to use your release is made by the station manager. Thus, it pays to make contact with this person. A visit to the local station enables you to meet the station manager and discuss ways in which you can work with the station. As an information agency within the community you have a lot to offer the station. For example, your library's

Figure 2.3   Special Event Public Service Announcement

Subject: Movie ("Desk Set")
Public service announcement to be used
Monday, May 7th through Tuesday, May 16th

Organization
and address: _____
_____

Contact: _____
(include your title _____
and phone number) _____

MOVIE: DESK SET, MAY 16th @ 8:00 P.M.

Announcement Time: 20 seconds
Number of Words: 51

ARE YOU A NOSTALGIA FAN? REMEMBER THOSE GREAT SPENCER TRACY, KATHERINE HEPBURN MOVIES? ONE OF THE BEST OF THEIR OLDIES—"DESK SET"— WILL BE SHOWN AT THE ROCK CITY PUBLIC LIBRARY ON TUESDAY EVENING MAY 16TH AT EIGHT IN THE EVENING. JOIN THE LOVERS OF YESTERYEAR AT THE MOVIE, "DESK SET."

reference department can provide background details to radio or TV reporters about events, or your library may contain a hard-to-find phonograph record that the station wants to use. Cooperation is an important element in developing an outlet for your message.

Your meeting with the station manager should provide information concerning format of releases and the type of material most likely to be broadcast. A tour of the facilities will give you a deeper insight into the workings of the station and emphasize your interest in a co-operative relationship. Assuming the role of listener or viewer, you can become familiar with the type of programming, the audience approach and the general character of the station.

When preparing your own public service announcement for the station, keep in mind what the listener or viewer can retain in 10, 20, 30 or 60 seconds. Limit your message to no more than two basic points. The rule of thumb for translating words into seconds for a radio announcement is:

10 seconds = 25 words	30 seconds = 75 words
15 seconds = 37 words	60 seconds = 150 words
20 seconds = 50 words	

When you write a public service message, it helps to use your library stationery. Use one sheet per release. Be sure your name, address and phone number are on the page. Include time limitations on the announcement. (You don't want a meeting announced the day after it is held.) Also, it helps to tell the announcer how many seconds the release will run when read on the air. Double or triple space your announcement.

In writing for the radio, keep in mind a few basic rules:

• Keep your sentences simple and your words descriptive.

• Stay away from words that are tongue-twisters or alliterative.

• Avoid long, no-pause sentences. Announcers like to breathe.

• Your initial words should be grabbers. Get the listener's attention first, then present the details of your message.

• Choose an informal and conversational style. Avoid being stiff or pedantic.

• If possible, repeat your message at least twice, using the same key words. A commercial for skin moisturizer repeats the name of the product eight times in 60 seconds.

• Don't overwrite. "Say it tight and make it right."

Finally, read the announcement to yourself—out loud. If you have a tape recorder, tape it and listen to the playback. Ask a colleague to comment on the message. Don't be afraid to rewrite, reread and retime until you have a script that delivers the message the way you want it.

Public service announcements are effective for promoting general library services, as well as specific events. Because they are not tied to a particular happening, they can be used at any time. Figure 2.4 illustrates sample messages of this type.

Figure 2.4   General Public Service Messages

20 seconds; 50 words
IF YOU'VE GIVEN UP READING BECAUSE BOOK PRINT IS TOO SMALL, LOOK AGAIN. YOUR LIBRARY HAS BEST SELLERS AND OLD FAVORITES IN THE LARGE PRINT FORMAT. AND YES, THEY'RE AS LIGHT IN WEIGHT AS REGULAR PRINT BOOKS. FOR YOUR READING PLEASURE VISIT THE PUBLIC LIBRARY FOR BOOKS IN LARGE PRINT.

10 seconds; 26 words
FIND OUT ABOUT BOOKS BY MAIL, A FREE SERVICE FOR PEOPLE LIVING IN RURAL AREAS. REGISTER AT YOUR NEAREST PUBLIC LIBRARY AND RECEIVE BOOKS BY MAIL.

15 seconds; 37 words
ENJOY VISITING MUSEUMS? EXTEND THE PLEASURE TO YOUR HOME, AT NO COST, BY BORROWING FRAMED ART REPRODUCTIONS FROM YOUR PUBLIC LIBRARY. REMBRANDT, CHAGALL, PICASSO, WINSLOW HOMER AND MANY OTHERS ARE WAITING FOR YOU. AT YOUR PUBLIC LIBRARY.

Source: Reprinted by permission of the author and publisher from Rita Kohn and Krysta Tepper, *You Can Do It: A PR Skills Manual for Librarians* (Metuchen, NJ: Scarecrow Press, Inc., 1981.) Copyright © 1981 by Rita Kohn and Krysta Tepper.

Preparing a Television Spot

If your community has a local broadcast or cable television outlet, another dimension is added to your library message—visual impact. This extra dimension means extra care has to be given to the choice of the message as well as to the method in which the message is presented. Obviously, a public service announcement with no visual impact potential should be avoided. Don't give up on television too quickly, however. A strong imagination can do wonders in developing visual images.

In most cases your message will not be a live or videotaped presentation, unless your library has access to video equipment and can produce its own tapes. A number of libraries own their own equipment, which they use for a wide variety of educational, informational and cultural programming; the same equipment may be used for public relations as well. In communities with cable TV franchises, libraries have access to use of one channel and often may receive instruction in the use of television equipment (see below).

However, still photos or color slides can also sell your message in a professional manner, assuming they are well shot and effectively organized. The most important aspect is still the message. Again, a tour of the local station and a meeting with the station manager or producer will open doors and provide you with information about the needs of the station. Don't be afraid to ask for help from station employees when you design your presentation.

There are a few basic differences between script preparation for radio and TV. The copy you write to accompany the visuals should be paced more slowly than radio copy because the viewer coordinates two senses—sight and sound. Thus, the ratio between words and seconds tightens. The TV ratio becomes:

10 seconds =   20 words
20 seconds =   40 words
60 seconds = 125 words

The script must be closely coordinated with visuals, but your copy must not simply duplicate what is shown. The exception is when you are illustrating an address or phone number. Music can be used providing it is well chosen. Background sound must not interfere with the basic message you are delivering. In selecting music, it is a wise idea to first check with the local station. Since recorded music is copyrighted you may discover that a fee may be due ASCAP (American Society of Composers, Authors and Publishers, 1 Lincoln Plaza, New York, NY 10023).

Using Cable TV

The laws pertaining to cable television are in a state of flux. At present, the cable company that has a franchise to operate in your area must provide a public access channel and a local government access channel. The library qualifies for use of the government channel. Groups or organizations that use the library's facilities for their own presentations qualify for public access use. In either case, local cable air time is readily accessible and offers the creative librarian the opportunity to take advantage of programs presented by others in the library or to actually produce library programs for the community.

Cable television requires some knowledge of equipment and TV technology. Many cable companies, as part of their franchise agreement with the city, are committed to educating the public on using video equipment. Thus, an individual or two, selected by the librarian, has the opportunity to take courses in TV operation. Often the franchise agreement also states that company equipment may be borrowed by trained individuals. Television tapes must be purchased by the library and, like audio tapes, can be used many times. Tape cost, however, is substantially higher—as much as $40 for a two-hour tape, compared to about $6 for an audio version.

Kinds of Programs

Types of programs that can be presented via television are as varied as the interests of the library's patrons. Programs may include story hours for children, public debates on community issues, panel groups discussing new books, instructional courses (these can cover cooking, languages, exercise, auto repair, estate planning—let your imagination be your guide) and, of course, interviews.

When selecting individuals for an interview or for potential course instructors, look to community resources first. It is always possible to go outside the community to hire people, but chances are your community has plenty of home-grown talent available. Keep a card file of residents and their special talents and interests. This is a good way to keep track of potential "guests." In most cases your speaker will volunteer his or her services at no cost. If the library is in a university community or within driving distance of a college, there will be a wealth of talent covering special disciplines. Don't forget to check with your local school system for possible topics and guests.

Another source of guests is the book publisher. All major publishing houses want their authors to receive publicity and often arrange speaking tours that take authors to nearby communities. A letter to the publicity director stating your plans to tape author interviews may well bring you an unexpected guest.*

Conducting a TV Interview

As for the interview itself, there are a few basics to consider. The odds are that your library staff contains neither a Barbara Walters nor a Mike Wallace. However, the individual you select as an interviewer must have many of the same qualities as a network star. Looks aren't important; confidence in oneself and an awareness of the subject under discussion are. The following guidelines may help.

• Do your homework. If you're talking about a book be sure you have read it. Some things can't be faked.

• Know the person you're interviewing. Some personal insights not only enable you to frame your questions more succinctly but also generate an aura of friendliness between interviewer and interviewee.

• Use graphics when possible. Television is a *visual* medium and two people sitting around a table talking can become dull unless the subject is extremely interesting. When interviewing an author, you must have a copy of the book. If you are dealing with a subject that can be illustrated (travel, current events, movies, art, etc.) try to obtain either still photographs or slides that can be used during the interview. Don't try to incorporate film footage unless you have the expertise to do so.

• Decide well before the interview what format you want to follow. Jot down both subject areas and specific questions. If you plan a half-hour interview have enough material prepared to cover an hour. However, once you start your interview allow the topic under discussion to lead you in your questioning process. There is nothing worse than reading a series of questions, many unrelated, and expecting the individual being interviewed to provide continuity for you. Your program will sound and look like a press conference. You can be assured that the interviewee will provide an answer that will enable you to follow up with a

---

*Publishers' names and addresses can be found in *Literary Market Place* (NY: R.R. Bowker & Co., annual) and *U.S. Book Publishing Yearbook and Directory 1981-82* (White Plains, NY: Knowledge Industry Publications, Inc., annual).

question not on your list. This is fine and provides the spark of spontaneity that holds an audience.

Interactive Television

The development of two-way, or interactive, cable television has considerable potential for libraries. Through such systems, coupled with computers, home viewers can have direct access to library information resources. Although few applications exist as yet, the Qube system in Columbus, OH, has been in operation since 1977. Using Qube, the Public Library of Columbus and Franklin County has produced a monthly television program, "Home Book Club," which allows viewers to "talk back" and respond to discussions of current bestsellers. At the end of each show, readers/viewers may participate in selecting the next book for discussion. Through the same Qube system, viewers can also request that the next book be mailed to their homes.

Ultimately the library plans to make a variety of information services, including reference materials, community information files and data bases, available to Qube subscribers. The opportunity for enhancing a library's service to and image in the community through such programming is enormous.

MAINTAINING GOOD PRESS RELATIONS

The library's relationship with newspapers, radio and television is a two-way, continuing process. The media are looking for news, the library for publicity. The library PR individual must not only make a good initial contact with an editor or station manager, but must maintain a cooperative association. Two long-established, productive relationships may illustrate this point.

The Roddenbery Memorial Library in Cairo, GA, has offered a Saturday morning "Pied Piper Story Hour," with stories told by staff members or college students, on local radio since 1948. The library also works hard to maintain a cooperative association with the local newspaper. Librarian Wessie Connell reports:

> We go the extra mile and initiate activities which engender good will. . . . For example, with our newspaper, we furnish extra columns or fillers not merely on library news but on things of interest to the entire area. When the annual Rattlesnake Round-Up is held in a neighboring community in February, the editor is furnished a fact sheet on snakes by the library, and in the fall during the hurricane season, fact sheets on weather and cyclones are furnished the paper. Occasionally we list titles of relevant books.[2]

Another example of well-maintained media relations comes from the experience of W. Best Harris, city librarian in Plymouth, England:

> We started our program at Plymouth with the one effective tool we had, a good local history department. We used this material to produce at least one weekly story for one or more of the local newspapers, stories not concerned with the functions of the library but with the contents of the library.

We made it our business—as we still do—to keep local reporters informed of such things as anniversaries of local events and personalities; of anything on the local history scene that was unusual, especially if it could be illustrated by an old print or photograph; and of any new acquisition of local flavor. Over a period of the first two years we got to know many of the local reporters, and through them we learned what constituted a story, and what a journalist would be looking for. Equally important, we gained their confidence and started the process of making them believe that libraries offered good copy from time to time. We backed up these local history press stories with illustrated lectures offered free to any organization anywhere in the city.[3]

These examples point up another aspect of marketing the library through the media: events do not have to be specifically library-oriented to be part of the library's PR effort. As the information service agency in your community, your mandate is very broad. By keeping aware of community activities and working with the media, the opportunity to spread the library's message widely, inexpensively and frequently is ever present.

THE NEWSLETTER

Newspaper, radio and television publicity represents an outsider's reportage of library activities; the newsletter represents the voice of the library. Many items not covered by the press can be dealt with in considerable detail in the newsletter. In large libraries, there may be a variety of in-house published newsletters, some aimed at library patrons, others at the library staff.

In the case of library systems, newsletters can be used to communicate to member libraries. In early 1980, for example, the Public Libraries Section of the New York Library Association initiated a quarterly newsletter, *Public Relations Plus,** to share public relations ideas, successes and failures. In its first issue the newsletter described how the Mamaroneck (NY) Free Library distributed paperbacks to motorists waiting in gas lines, how another library helped to save the local newspaper and other activities.

In-house newsletters can also assist in educating staff members, informing them of changes in the library, policy matters and technical data. When the Chicago Public Library was in the process of converting to an automated circulation system, it launched a newsletter, *Data Processing News,* to keep staff members up-to-date on the progress of the switch-over as well as its implications. The newsletter is described as "a forum for communication, information, and problem exchange, new ideas and solutions." The library plans to keep publishing not only for the duration of the project but "for as long as we are growing and evolving into new and different forms of computer-assisted information access."[4]

Newsletters designed for the community must be informative, attractive and nontechnical. Avoid library jargon and the common buzz words so familiar to the professional librarian. Staff news should be omitted. Details on the workings of the library are also inappropriate, unless there is a change that will have a direct effect on the patron.

---

*Available free from: Public Information Department, Mid-Hudson Library System, 103 Market St., Poughkeepsie, NY 12601.

Before starting a newsletter, there are a few basic questions that should be considered:

• Assuming you have a need to communicate more effectively, is a newsletter the answer?

• If you are planning an in-house newsletter, will it be cost-effective?

• Will the information provided by the newsletter supplant or complement staff meetings?

• Is there enough money in the library budget to cover the cost of a newsletter? Are outside funds available to help defray costs?

• Is there enough information to justify a newsletter on a continuing basis?

The Role of the Editor

Once the decision is made to commit library or outside funds to a publications program, the next major decision is who will be responsible for overseeing the project. Someone who is interested, motivated and able to do the best job possible is needed. This individual, or editor, must have the full support and backing of the library director. Although the editor is usually a staff member, there is no reason why a reliable volunteer couldn't handle the job. The duties and responsibilities of the editor must be clearly understood by the director as well as the other librarians. The editor's job description must provide the responsibility and *authority* to set deadlines, solicit articles, arrange for photo sessions and make final decisions. Since money must be spent the editor must have a budget and the authority to use it.

The same qualities specified for the public relations specialist are needed by the newsletter editor. The editor must oversee, compile, write, edit, type and be prepared to be directly involved with the printing or mimeo process. A lot of busy work is involved: folding, stapling, stuffing envelopes, taking material to a printer, post office or film lab. In other words, the editor, too, wears many hats and is involved in many activities never suggested at library school.

The type and quality of information included in the newsletter demands an openminded editor who understands the needs of the community and the library. As editor, the material covered must interest you or it won't interest others. An editor who concentrates on human events and activities is in a better position to capture the interest of the audience. Whether editing for an in-house audience or a large community one, the editor must have a clear picture of the audience.

Some specific story ideas that can be included in a newsletter have been suggested by Sally Brickman, of Case Western Reserve University Libraries:[5]

• Getting to know you—highlight staff and its accomplishments.

• Meetings and programs—when they are, who will speak, what issues. Follow-up in the next newsletter.

• Building plans.

• Book reviews, new and old books, book sales and interlibrary loan.

• What's new in library literature, organizations, papers and people.

• Letters from happy patrons and their suggestions; columns by the director and a roving reporter.

• Policy changes and new services.

• Consumer education, how-to articles, legislation.

• Special services: microfilm, microfiche, equipment available for rental, video tape programs, etc.

• *Avoid* personal issues about staff and patrons.

Budget Planning

Before starting a newsletter, determine well in advance the size of the newsletter, amount of copy or pictures required, the cost of printing or using the mimeograph machine and the cost of distribution. These elements will enable you to plan a budget. It's a good idea to add at least 10% to the final budget figure to cover inflation. In particular, the price of paper is rising at a rapid rate.

A hidden cost that many people erroneously consider part of the printing process is that of typesetting. Professional typesetting charges vary enormously; a minimum is about $15 per page. Some libraries own word processing equipment with typesetting features or may have access to word processors owned by other local organizations. The use of word processors simplifies editing and produces a professional looking newsletter at considerable savings. However, libraries without such equipment can still produce attractive and interesting "typography" by using a typewriter with interchangeable heads.

The format of the newsletter—physical size and number of columns—can vary according to the tastes of the editor. Most newsletters use an 8½-inch by 11-inch page. This will provide two columns of approximately 3¼ inches each or three columns of about 2¼ inches each. Photos can be contained in a single column or spread across several columns depending on the layout of the designer. Major stories can be run in two columns (using a three-column format), giving added importance to your message. If both sides of a standard 8½-inch by 11-inch sheet are used, there is room for about 1200 to 2000 words of copy (depending on type size), a logo or masthead and a blank one-third page for affixing an address and postage. If the newsletter is not to be mailed, this third of a page is used for additional copy.

With a printed newsletter, you can double the size without doubling the cost (although some increased cost will be incurred). To produce a four-page publication, each page 8½ by 11 inches, the printer uses a single sheet of paper measuring 8½ by 17 inches. The sheet is printed and folded in half. It is usually folded again in the shape of a folded business letter. The final publication can now be mailed in a standard number 10 envelope or used as a self-mailer.

Printing costs vary, of course, but are based on several factors, including the size of the newsletter, the quality of paper selected, the number of copies desired, and the number of colors used. When photographs are used, a glossy paper is more desirable than the less expensive bond. Newsprint is the least expensive. In estimating costs, the printer uses a fixed standard for his setup charges. These include making plates, preparing photos, inking the press and cleaning up the press after the print run. These setup charges are constant regardless of the number of copies run. Therefore, it is cheaper, on a per unit basis, to print a large number of copies.

Before choosing a printer, shop around and obtain comparative prices. The cost of printing varies greatly by region as well as by individual printers within the same region. Table 2.1 reflects typical costs for printing an 8½- by 11-inch sheet of 20 pound white bond paper.

Table 2.1: Typical Newsletter Printing Costs

Number of Copies	1 color 1 side	1 color 2 sides	2 color 1 side	2 color on 1 side & 1 color on reverse side
1,000	$ 28	$ 51	$ 60	81
5,000	92	151	171	227
10,000	171	287	302	401

Source: Based on author's survey of printers in the New York area, June 1981.

One possible way to save money once you have decided on a printer is to offer to buy a six month or one year supply of paper in advance. Not only do you offset the increase in future paper prices, but you may get a discount by buying paper in bulk. These cost savings, however, must make up for the potential loss of income incurred by tying up your assets for this period of time.

Newsletter Design

The design of the newsletter is another important element. Since the newsletter is the representative of the library, it must portray the library in its best light. The newsletter must strive to obtain its own identity. This can be accomplished by the use of a well-designed masthead or logo. An eye-catching design is not easy to achieve. A simple, uncluttered look works best. Often, a local designer can be asked to develop a newsletter design on a voluntary or low-cost basis.

Instead of a formal design used as a logo, consider a photo or drawing of the library, an open book, the initials of the library arranged in an interesting pattern, etc. If an attractive masthead is used, there is no reason why a logo has to be included. The prime purpose of the design element is to draw attention to your product (the newsletter) and to assure recognition.

The use of a colored ink is another way to reinforce recognition, and the cost of colored ink is minimal. One major consideration, however, should be kept in mind: any photos used in the newsletter will appear in the same color as the ink selected. Also remember that certain colors have a negative effect on readability. Avoid reds and light colors against a white paper. Consider using color to highlight your logo and masthead—then print your body copy (including photos) in black. Keep in mind, however, that a two-color selection will increase printing costs since each sheet must be fed through the press twice—once for each color.

The masthead should include your library's name, location, volume, number and date. The newsletter title (*Library Views, Book News, Bookmark,* etc.) should be given the most prominence. (See Figure 2.5.)

If an experienced designer is not available, experiment with several styles and layouts before committing yourself to a final format. Try different arrangements incorporating boxes, borders, symbols and pictures. Drawings can be used as well as photographs. If you do select photographs, make them interesting. Show people in action. There is nothing duller than an individual standing next to a stack of books.

In preparing copy, apply the same basic rules for writing a press release. Start off with a catchy lead sentence. Get the reader's attention with your initial paragraph. Keep your paragraphs short, and try to eliminate unnecessary words. A headline, written as a complete sentence, is another attention getter. It's a good idea to read your own copy first, but another proofreading should be done by someone else. Check spelling, grammar and punctuation. A dictionary and thesaurus are good companions. A style manual is also helpful.

Distribution

In the original newsletter concept you undoubtedly had a specific audience in mind. Reaching that audience and delivering the finished, printed newsletter is another matter.

Distribution methods depend on the type of newsletter, size of the library budget and the nature and size of the community. A newsletter need not be mailed; personal distribution in the library can work very well. There should be a central distribution point where newsletters and other printed material (book marks, film schedules, policy statements, schedule of coming events, etc.) are readily available and highly visible. The circulation desk is an excellent place to distribute printed material. Often the librarian checking out books can sug-

Figure 2.5   Newsletter with an Eye-catching Masthead from the White Plains (NY) Public Library

DIRECTIONS

NEWS OF THE WHITE PLAINS LIBRARY   **SUMMER 1981 / NO. 16**

The Pied Pipers!

(l-r) Sandy Sivulich, Gigi Avitabile, Lee Palmer, Jo Carpenter, Sara Miller (not pictured, Florence Modell, Edith Carpentieri).

Children love the warm and welcoming place that is the Children's Library, a world filled with books, records, toys to borrow, magazines and special things to do. What draws them back again and again is the unique group of people that makes up the staff — special people who are their special friends.

Sara Miller, who for eight years has been the head of children's services, is the catalyst that sparks this group. She has received professional recognition for her knowledge of children's literature and recently served a term as a member of the prestigious Newbery Medal Committee, which each year selects the best in children's books. She gives classes at Pace University and Manhattanville's Graduate School. Sara received her MLS from Columbia, and worked for several years at New York Public Library, serving a valuable apprenticeship with their eminent children's coordinator, Augusta Baker. She takes special pride in the "Alice Room," a research collection for serious students of children's literature, teachers, authors and illustrators, which houses landmark and prize winning children's books and reference material. Among her pet projects have been workshops on successful parenting and introducing children to books. Schoolchildren welcome her class visits, as she brings the many aspects of the Library to life and tells about the many marvelous activities she and the staff plan and present. "But" she says, "all these extras are icing on the cake, planned with only one goal in mind — to put a child and a book together!"

Librarian **Florence Modell** has that special flair for putting a child with just the right book. She received her MLS from Queens, after taking time out to raise her family, worked for a time as a school librarian and came to White Plains thirteen years ago.

Her love of children's books is contagious and she is as thorough as she is enthusiastic. A youngster who has an assignment on the Soviet Union will be led to books on Russian art, music, folklore and cooking, as well as fiction and background. Her "specialty" is books for the very young. She tells us, "Nothing is too good for a child. The best picture books are a blend of fine art and rhythmic prose." Among her "must reads" are the classic Goodnight Moon by Margaret Wise Brown, Beatrix Potter's The Tale of Peter Rabbit and Maurice Sendak's The Nutshell Library.

The newest member of the Children's Room Staff is **Sandy Sivulich,** who joined us as a part-time librarian in 1979. She received her MLS from Rosary College in River Forest, Ill., and worked in the Chicago area where she was active in professional library associations. Sandy, who has also served on the Newbery Medal Committee, taught children's literature and did hospital storytelling and library consulting in Erie, Pa., before moving here with her husband and small daughter two years ago. She particularly enjoys traditional storytelling, and has given workshops for parents, nursery

school teachers and weekend storytellers in games, fingerplays and storytelling. Her Sunday Story Times, where youngsters bring teddy bears, rag dolls and stuffed animals are weekend highlights. A perennial favorite is her own version of I'm Going On A Bear Hunt (published by E.B. Dutton in 1973) where the youngsters "swim," "row" and "climb" with her through rough terrain to find that bear!

When youngsters enjoy our popular puppet shows, they are entertained by a talented team who, it's hard to believe, have 43 years of Children's Room experience among them!

Author and puppeteer **Lee Palmer's** job title reads "Storyteller," and she is the only official staff storyteller in Westchester. Young alumni of her popular Story Times who meet her in the supermarket or on the street are amazed to realize she doesn't live in her special purple chair in the Story Room, picture book in hand. Fifteen years ago, while working as a PTA volunteer in the Ridgeway School Library, she took a storytelling course at the Library and was asked to come on staff for "twenty minutes

(Pied-Pipers, continued p.2)

gest that the latest newsletter or other pertinent piece of literature be taken along with the armload of books. Another common location to distribute literature is at the library's entrance. A large slotted stand or table can be placed there to attract the attention of all who enter and leave the library.

On the other hand, selective mailings are very effective and increase the community's awareness of the library. Selecting the mailing list requires judgment. The cost of mailing is the single most expensive item in most newsletter publishing ventures. Even though the library qualifies for a special, nonprofit postage rate, bulk mailing still costs a few cents per recipient.

There are a few individuals and groups who should definitely be on your list. Certainly, any individual who specifically requests a copy should be included, as should members of a Friends of the Library organization. It is also a good idea to add key individuals in the community whose influence is important to the library. These should include all local government leaders, officers of local civic organizations, other libraries (including school, corporate and private) in the community and regional library organizations. Make sure all members of the library staff receive their personal copy—public relations begins at home.

It is a good idea to consider at least one communitywide mailing a year. If the community is a small one then you probably will be sending your newsletter to every family. In large cities and towns, this will probably be too expensive. However, by using a coupon or return card you can test local interest in your newsletter. Simply request those who want a free subscription to return the coupon. Coupons should also be easily accessible in the library.

Your list of subscribers should also include all cardholders. One problem is that there is usually more than one cardholder to a family. Sending multiple copies of the newsletter to a single address is expensive and can create a negative image. If possible, a special mailing list of cardholders should be prepared annually with the newsletter addressed to the "Smith Family."

Lists can be typed on special forms which, when used in most duplicating machines, will produce pressure-sensitive labels. Although this method requires a great deal of hand labor, it is probably more cost-effective than using computer-generated labels. If you plan to use several lists, be sure to code them to avoid duplication of mailings. For community-wide mailings, it is usually too expensive to prepare a special list of all families in your area. A call to the town, village or city clerk's office should let you know whether the list you need is already available. Since all municipalities have their own lists for tax purposes, it is possible to borrow or rent a computerized set of labels.

Locating apartment dwellers is another matter. Companies that sell mailing lists may be able to assist in assembling names of community members not available through the clerk's office. These list brokers will charge from $40 to $75 per thousand names. Often you may acquire a list of apartment houses by zip code rather than individual names. The list broker may suggest that the slug "occupant" or "resident" be used. These slugs are also computer-generated and can be included in the standard price, or are available at a slight additional charge. (See also Chapter 5.)

Scheduling

Consideration must also be given to timing publication and mailing. If a special event is planned at the library, you should plan your mailing to assure maximum publicity. You should avoid sending your newsletter in the midst of the Christmas season, for example, when it can easily be lost under a pile of greeting cards. The summer is another time to avoid if many members of the community are away on vacation. In many areas of the country the first week of a month is "bill week." The psychological disadvantage of having your newsletter delivered with a host of bills should also be considered.

Once the decision is made as to the frequency of publication, it is important to hold to your schedule. If people know when to expect the newsletter they will begin to look forward to receiving library information on an established schedule. Scheduling also makes it much easier for the newsletter's editor to assign articles, edit and plan printing and mailing.

Funding the Newsletter

Funding the newsletter is always an important consideration during these times of tight budgets and high interest rates. Consider community fundraising efforts for the sole purpose of publishing a newsletter. Money from a library book fair, sale of books that have been weeded from the collection, or library special events for which an admission fee is charged are other possible fundraising options. Perhaps the most common source of funds for newsletters is a Friends of the Library group.

Before seeking money from the Friends, the community or any civic group, it is important to determine in advance a full year's costs. A full budget, with costs spread out on a month-by-month basis, should be prepared. Since there will be little, if any, editorial costs involved, major expenditures will be for printing and mailing. These costs can be estimated quite accurately once you have established the number of copies to be printed and the number to be mailed. These amounts won't be identical since you will want a supply of newsletters in the library to be used as handouts. Include in your cash estimate the following costs: list rental, indicia (plus annual mail permit), envelopes if a self-mailer is not used, mailing house charges for affixing labels and stuffing envelopes, postage and a miscellaneous category that covers items such as film, pencils, pens, typewriter ribbons, photocopying charges, posterboards for preparing mechanicals, etc.

THE ANNUAL REPORT

Another publication that enables the library to get its message across to the public is the annual report. Its purpose, design, theme and audience vary greatly. For some, the annual report is published for the edification of a specialized public—trustees, library staff and legislators. For others, the report is another way to reach patrons and nonlibrary users with the message that the public library is a community resource operated by a dedicated group of information specialists. In addition, the report serves as a vehicle of accountability to the public.

What is the library doing with public funds? How is the taxpayer benefiting? The report gives the library the chance to pat itself on the back. In the process of telling the public what a good job the library is doing, the report can also increase staff pride in its work.

Establishing a Theme

Many annual reports contain basic circulation data from the previous year, number of new library cards issued, reference calls received, etc. However, there are also many annual reports that are based around a central theme. A new building addition, an important anniversary, the retirement of a major community public figure, or the need for new services or important equipment can serve as themes. Other themes cover goals and accomplishments of the previous year or aspirations for the forthcoming year, recent major acquisitions, new programs, community involvement, etc. The theme should be expressed by the title, and carried out consistently throughout the text.

Some interesting themes have been found in the annual reports of public libraries in recent years. The Public Library of Youngstown and Mahoning County (OH) published an annual report entitled "Thanks to Everyone," basing its theme around a successful library fundraising effort. A report published by the Hunterdon County Library, Flemington, NJ was entitled "Yours for only $2.38." The theme referred to the per capita tax revenue spent by community members on library services.

It is helpful to review what other libraries are doing, so send for copies of annual reports published by neighboring libraries as well as libraries of comparable sizes in other parts of the country. Also look at the annual reports published by business organizations. Obviously, the public library can little afford the luxury of a lavish, four-color report like those produced by IBM, General Motors or Eastman Kodak. However, the ideas expressed in both style and coverage may be worth considering. For example, the Harland Co., which supplies checks and checkbooks to bank customers, designed its annual report in the shape and format of a wallet-sized checkbook. A library's annual report can show the same imagination. The New Orleans Public Library, in a city renowned for its French restaurants, recently designed its annual report to resemble the menu of an elegant New Orleans restaurant. (See Figure 2.6.)

Most library public relations specialists have developed the theme of an annual report well in advance of production time. Ideas can spring from meetings with staff members, the director, trustees, Friends or from reports published by other libraries. It helps to develop an idea file or folder in which you can place random bits of useful information accumulated over the year. Collect attractive layouts from brochures and pamphlets, unusual reference questions, letters or phone calls from patrons that highlight various aspects of library services, library statistics, photographs taken in the library, etc.

The annual report should emphasize the major aspects of your library's services—the collection, personnel, individuals and groups served, special events and activities. When you mention staff, board or community participation in library activities, you are emphasizing community awareness of the library and the services it performs.

Figure 2.6   Front Cover and Sample Page from the New Orleans Public Library
Annual Report

MENU

APPETIZERS

Art Exhibit Quiche
Central Library and branches showcase original work
by artists in the community, providing an outlet
through which patrons can become familiar with the
art and culture of their communities.

Women's Night Canape
A weekly forum addressin g women's issues and
interests through programs of cultural, political,
social and personal significance. Both men and
women are invited to participate.

Tossed Afro-American History Month
This Bicentennial February exploded with a Black
Experience Film Festival at four library locations,
a lecture series at one branch, Dashiki and Free
Southern Theatre performances, and Danny Barker and
his jazz band at all library locations.

Securities and Investing (in season)
Popular lecture and discussion series conducted
by local stockbrokers held at various library
locations.

Lump Open House Cocktail
The Central Library opened its doors one Sunday in
May to an afternoon of continuous programming on
all three floors simultaneously. This event was
designed to highlight, through live presentation,
the varied resources of the NOPL.

Marinated French Arts Festival
Algiers Regional Branch hosted a month-long
festival of weekly films, concerts and slide-lectures,
immersing patrons in the historic culture of France.

Films du Jour with Chitterlings
Full-length Shakespeare films, The Six Wives of
Henry VIII, The Spoils of Poynton, a weekly lunch
hour film festival at Central, and films for children
were offered throughout the system.

Producing the Report

The production schedule for the annual report will be determined mainly by the intended date of publication. This is often timed to coincide with the library's annual meeting or the beginning of a fiscal year.

The amount of time required to produce the report will vary with the number of staff members available to work on the project, the size of the report and the budget. The Public Library of Cincinnati and Hamilton County (OH) starts two months prior to publication date. The production of the Lorain (OH) Public Library annual report takes Betty Piper, public relations specialist, about "one month, from my conference with the director to finished copy. But I work on other things between times too."[6]

The size, design and number of copies produced will depend in large part on the size of your budget. Often the Friends or a business organization in the community will sponsor the annual report. If these outside funds are not available, costs must be paid from the library's public relations budget. The same cost considerations that apply to newsletter production, previously discussed, apply here. Remember that the message is most important and that a simple report can serve the purpose. It isn't necessary to produce an annual report in the style of A.T.&T.

In designing the annual report, keep in mind that a cluttered page will lose your audience quickly. Keep your presentation uncomplicated. A simple cover and brief headlines with a few large illustrations may be all that is required to capture the reader's attention. Avoid in-house library jargon such as loan transactions, search techniques, interlibrary loan, COM, LC, etc. By preparing the copy in advance, it is much easier to plan a layout. Cutting material if the layout is too tight is simpler than adding "puff" that fools no one and will dilute your message.

Distributing the Report

A good looking annual report has little, if any, impact if it is not distributed to the core audience that is so important to the library. This group should include members of the library board, city council or other local government officials, advisory committees, Friends, staff and, of course, your users. Other groups to consider include community leaders, state and federal legislators, executives of major corporations in the area, and representatives of local schools and other educational institutions. Since the individuals on your core list may fluctuate periodically, your list should be reviewed each time your annual report is published.

In addition to supplying information to the core group and community, the annual report also provides an excellent opportunity for press releases to local papers and radio/TV stations. A copy of the report should accompany the release, and it should be stated that extra copies of the report are available at no charge from the library. It is also possible to increase public awareness of the report and the library by offering extra copies of your annual report to such individuals and organizations as clubs, supermarkets, banks, doctors and local realtors. If your community has a Welcome Wagon, copies of the annual report, as well as other library publications, should be made available.

CONCLUSION

The library's marketing specialist must take advantage of all available resources to communicate with patrons and all members of the community who influence the library's future. The use of press releases, newsletters, radio and TV announcements and annual reports are among these resources. Although cost must be a factor in deciding how best to spread the word, the cost to the library of failing to sell its services may be far higher. Chapter 3 will offer some guidelines in the use of other marketing techniques, the development of special programs and displays.

FOOTNOTES

1. Edward J. Montana Jr., "Public Relations for the Metropolitan Library," in *Public Relations for Libraries*, ed. Allan Angoff (Westport, CT: Greenwood Press, 1973), p. 19.

2. Wessie Connell, "Public Relations in the Small Public Library," in *Public Relations for Libraries*, ed. Allan Angoff (Westport, CT: Greenwood Press, 1973), p. 78.

3. W. Best Harris, "Public Relations for Public Libraries," *Assistant Librarian* 64 (February 1971): 18.

4. *Library Journal* 105 (February 15, 1980): 2370.

5. "Prepare: The Library Public Relations Recipe Book," mimeographed (Preconference publication of the Public Relations Section, Library Administration Division, American Library Association, 1978), p. 9.

6. Ibid., p. 41.

3

Special Programs and Events

In addition to marketing through the media, libraries have numerous on-site methods of attracting public support. These include special exhibits and displays; programs such as children's story hours, films, lectures and discussion groups; book fairs; and generation of bibliographies geared to special interests.

EXHIBITS AND DISPLAYS

What is the first impression a patron has when walking into your library? Does he run smack into a sign saying "Please close the door!" or a drab, crowded circulation desk? In too many libraries, first impressions are often negative, despite the best intentions of the library director. (Imagine walking into someone's home and being greeted by a statement requesting you not to smoke or not to park your car where you did.) Consider how much better you would feel walking into your library and discovering a poster, sign or display that made you smile or provoked your curiosity. (See Figure 3.1.) There is no reason why *any* library cannot produce a display near the entrance that serves to welcome or inform a patron.

Although any exhibit or display must be an attractive addition to the library, it must also sell. The product being sold in most cases is information. According to Mona Garvey, Public Relations/Educational Display Consultant and president of M.G. Associates, Atlanta, GA, "The first purpose of library displays is to assist the patron in use of the library. This purpose often gets lost in the pursuit of splashy seasonal and holiday displays, but it is, or should be, the starting point of display planning—and *displaying* should be a planned, scheduled activity rather than a haphazard filling of available space."[1]

A public display usually offers suggestions about library materials or services in which a patron might be interested. Attractive bulletin boards, top-of-the-catalog displays or simple posters all serve to inform. Although it is important that the display be attractive, there is

Figure 3.1   A Promotional Poster

Source: American Library Association. Reproduced with permission.

sometimes the danger of becoming too "arty." Remember that the purpose of the exhibit is to "sell" the books and information projected to the viewers. The librarian can sometimes create a pretty picture, even one fit for a museum, but it may not motivate sufficient reader interest to request the material presented. If this is the case, the display has failed. On the other hand, a crudely lettered sign that looks like the third-prize winner in an elementary school art contest will be equally unsuccessful.

Use Your Imagination

The following are only a sample of imaginative signs and displays that have brought positive responses at libraries throughout the country.

• At New York City's Cooper Union for Advancement of Science and Art library, a sign placed in a window stated, "The $64.00 Answer." Beneath the sign the director had assembled $64.15 worth of books that would supply the average reader with answers to questions on a very wide range of subjects.

• The Salina (KS) Public Library, working with a local publisher, produced a display illustrating the various stages in producing a book jacket from initial design to finished printed version.

• Publishers were only too willing to cooperate with the Public Library of Youngstown and Mahoning County (OH) in developing its display, "Book Forecast." Dust jackets of soon-to-be-published books were supplied by publishers to alert patrons to forthcoming titles. Patrons could leave reserves for the books and were pleased that they were privy to the latest news of the season's coming books. The library also received another benefit. The exhibit helped overcome the notion that "the library never has any new books."

• If you visit the public library in Janesville, WI, right before Easter, don't be surprised to see a display of a children's Easter egg competition.

• The public library in Barrington, RI, did not intend to be sexist when it conceived a "Men Only" hobby show. The library felt that women's hobbies are quite familiar but few people know how men spend their spare time. The exhibit opened with refreshments prepared by a male member of the library board whose hobby was cooking. Men served tea, assisted by boys from the local junior and senior high schools. The event was the library's most popular exhibit of the year.

• Combining library books with a special exhibit is a common and effective technique. In Trinidad, West Indies, the public library displayed books on handicrafts, then exhibited specific examples of each craft made by local members of the community. Crafts and their corresponding how-to books were divided into weaving, basketry and cane work, embroidery and needlework, woodwork, crochet and knitting, music, artificial flowers, leatherwork, carving, toys, Christmas cards, etc.

As the above examples illustrate, themes for an exhibit can vary tremendously. Pick a book from your library's shelf and a theme should come to mind. Consider the various weeks or months that have been declared by a state or the federal government as "special." National Secretary's Week, National Dairy Month, Flower Week, Solar Day and, naturally, National Library Week are among the possibilities. For example, a library might plan an exhibit of special Bibles for Bible Week. The exhibit could include Bibles of interest borrowed from community members or neighboring libraries. Both the Library of Congress and the National Archives in Washington, DC have interesting facsimiles of rare book pages, maps, and art works available at a low cost. Catalogs and listings of their materials are available. All it takes is a little imagination.

Cooperative Exhibits

The display need not be in the library to catch the public's attention and sell the library's message. Marie D. Loizeaux describes how Baltimore's Enoch Pratt Free Library used existing window space to promote library services and suggests "borrowing" a window in a local store. One eye-catching idea is the use of travel posters. "They are so colorful and strong in design that the effect is almost always good. One travel poster and a dozen books make a perfectly satisfactory window display that can be changed frequently with great ease and endless variety."[2] Keep in mind, however, that if the window is some distance from the library, directions or a simple map must be included to give window-watchers the answer to their first question: How do I get to the library?

Locating an available window in the community may not be difficult. Local realtors are prime candidates to "donate" a window: it's in their interest to sell the value of the community to their customers. What better way than to promote the features of the local library? They may also know of another store with an available window.

In the spring a local hardware merchant might donate his window for a few weeks for an exhibit of garden literature, along with the store's latest assortment of seeds or garden implements. In addition, you may ask the merchant to exhibit some of his wares at the library in conjunction with your book exhibit. A local grocer or supermarket may be willing to lend you his window for a week or two in exchange for a display in the library of cook books and grocery items. A short notice acknowledging the source of the items—e.g., "Gardening implements courtesy of ABC Hardware"—should be placed with the library display. (The library should not appear to be advertising the storekeeper's merchandise, and there should be no reference to the quality, price, availability, etc. of the goods on display.)

When properly approached, almost any store owner will welcome the opportunity to work with the library as a matter of self-interest. It may take a bit of salesmanship on the part of the library, but the results will be of lasting benefit.

Cooperative exhibits, whether in or out of the library, have many associated benefits. The local garden club, historical society, gourmet club, PTA, etc. are usually most interested in displaying the fruits of their members' labors. And what better place to display a hooked rug or new watercolor than the local library? Recently neighborhood banks have joined the 20th century and realized that public relations and community good will pay off. Libraries should learn from the experience of these banks. Exhibits of residents' photographs, paintings, handicrafts or sculpture are now common in banks. Why not in the library? One large savings bank in New York City has an annual fashion show in the fall and a dog show in February. The cost of producing these shows is relatively small, but the public relations value and customer interest is immense.

If there is a local author in the community or a neighboring town, you might arrange an autograph party with copies of the author's book on display. Publishers need libraries and publicity and are likely to be cooperative. The Enoch Pratt Free Library in Baltimore frequently devotes an entire window to a single new volume of a local author. Thirty copies of the work are borrowed from the publisher along with original art, if any, and a photograph of the author to add a personal touch.

Local publishers are particularly likely to be helpful in supplying books and related materials for a display. It should be noted that the days in which New York was the sole publishing hub of the nation is no longer true. Today, there are more publishers in business than ever before, and they are scattered throughout the country. *Literary Market Place* lists publishers both alphabetically and regionally. Another source, the *U.S. Book Publishing Yearbook and Directory,* lists publishers alphabetically and includes the names and numbers of various contacts in each firm. The listing of book publishers in *Books in Print* contains many more small, regional publishers that are not listed in *Literary Market Place.* Another source of local publishers is the Yellow Pages of your local phone directory.

SETTING UP THE DISPLAY

Whatever subject you select for your exhibit, the way in which the display is presented has a lot to do with its effect.

Design Considerations

The use of color is an important consideration. Tones should harmonize or contrast, not clash. In the summer consider the cooler colors—blue, green, gray and white. During the winter months the warmer colors would predominate—red, yellow, orange, etc. Colorful posters, picture maps and book jackets are valuable not only for their intrinsic value but for their ability to catch the eye of the passerby.

When selecting books for display, pick books that can be shown to their best advantage —readable spines in good condition, attractive covers and illustrations, clear easy-to-read print are factors to consider. When displaying book jackets, wrap them around an existing book rather than show them alone. Old books that are unlikely to circulate are good for this purpose.

All your exhibits, whether in a display case, store window or bulletin board, should have a backdrop that is eye catching. A colored fabric can be used in display cases as well as on bulletin boards. Another material that works well is wallboard, or portable light-weight panels that are reinforced with wooden frames to prevent warping. These panels can be painted with quick-drying water-base paint. They can be made self-supporting with the addition of small wooden feet at the base of the panel.

The exhibit must be considered as a whole. The best conceived display will be weakened considerably by an unattractive sign or poorly lettered captions. Posters, signs and showcards used in the exhibit must supplement each other. As a total unit they tell the library's story and carry your message. One common mistake made in the marriage of words and art is the belief that every bit of space must be used. Openness or white space is an important design element and should be encouraged. Libraries lacking a competent staff or volunteer artist may want to consider investing in an enlarging projector (similar to an overhead projector, but with enhanced capabilities) for enlarging or reducing special illustrations in the collection. Lettering devices, stencils and various "stick-on" letters are available from a local art supply store. The most durable form of letters are die-cut from a variety of materials. These range from thin Mutual Aids, adhesive and non-adhesive, to the thicker Hallcraft, Redicut, etc.

Lighting

Lighting is another important element to consider in planning the exhibit. All the hours of work and planning will be meaningless unless your patrons can see your exhibit clearly and without distraction. Few libraries are equipped with the modern type of display lighting for proper presentation of an exhibit. It is often necessary to supplement existing electrical facilities with temporary installations to present an exhibit in its best light.

Many electric power companies will provide free advice to libraries in determining electrical requirements or suggest ways to highlight an exhibit to its best advantage. Various studies have shown that an item in a supermarket will sell several times faster to impulse buyers when displayed on a special spot-lighted fixture than it does in its regular place on the shelf. This same principle of attracting "buyers" is also valid in the library. Generally, the brightness or quantity of light reflected should be from two to five times that of the surrounding area in order to attract attention.

If possible, avoid placing very dark and very light objects close to each other if they are equally important to a lighted display. For example, a book jacket decorated with a glossy black background featuring heavy, blue lettering is an eye-catching cover in itself. Place this jacket beside a book with a pastel-colored jacket and both books lose their individual eye appeal. If one of these books is spotlighted, however, a good effect can be achieved.

Selecting special spots or bulbs can be an art. Fluorescent lamps produce two to three times as many units of light per watt as do incandescent bulbs. Thus, they are often preferred in exhibit cases or other confined spaces where heat presents a problem. Since all incandescent lamps create a great deal of heat, they must be used sparingly. Heat can be damaging to vellum, ivories, leather, painted and illuminated pages, as well as many forms of wooden structures that may dry out in the absence of moisture in the atmosphere.

Another problem that should be considered is the potential glare that many types of bulbs and reflectors can create. Reflection off glass cases can be a particular problem in creating a proper lighting design. Fluorescent lamps have the advantage of coolness, but lack the variety and intensity that can be obtained from incandescent lamps. Trying to obtain true colors with fluorescent light can present quite a headache. In the late 1950s a "soft white" tube was developed to counteract the problems associated with early fluorescent illumination —yellow, orange and red tones were distorted. The "soft white" lamp solved this specific problem but because of its pinkish hue, created others. Today, it is possible to buy fluorescent light that does not distort color as much as it did in the past. However, incandescent light is still superior for preserving color tones accurately.

Because of the potential problems that can occur in showcase lighting, it is recommended that an individual with some degree of expertise be consulted. Professional stage lighting designers are available in many cities. In areas that have an active school drama department, try the drama teacher who must deal with stage lighting problems.

AUDIOVISUAL DISPLAYS

Audiovisual displays are also worth considering for library use. Slide presentations can be synchronized with an audio tape to provide an exciting sight and sound program. The expertise required to produce a slide-tape show is not excessive, thanks to modern cameras that do everything but snap the shutter. The types of programs are almost limitless. An AV program can be shown to community groups for a variety of promotion purposes including: a budget report, building expansion, annual gift solicitation, new collection of books or periodicals, forthcoming lecture or movie, book fair, etc.

If you are planning an elaborate AV display, it is wise to call on an experienced consultant for help. Also consider the possibility of sharing your exhibit with a neighboring library. Such potential reciprocity not only enhances the number and variety of exhibits you can plan, but leads to additional cooperative ventures between libraries. Often, the state or county library system will have a cooperative program in existence. System-wide motion picture collections are common. A growing trend among library systems is the collection and sharing of video cassettes, including tapes of programs originally broadcast over the air.

One potential problem of off-the-air taping of existing programs and the lending of these cassettes to patrons is the danger of copyright infringement. To date, libraries have not been involved in copyright violation suits involving video taping. However, like the cases involving distribution of photocopies of periodicals and book pages, a video copyright infringement suit is simply a question of time.

ADMINISTRATIVE CONSIDERATIONS

Often the individual responsible for public relations lacks the time, talent or both to plan and execute the library's public displays. However, a staff member may have the desire and potential talent to work with the public relations coordinator in this effort. Perhaps a volunteer from the community could be found through a notice in the library or the local newspaper. Regardless of how the individual or individuals are obtained, the development and implementation of a display program is an important segment of the library's overall "selling" concept and must be carefully planned, organized and controlled. One individual, responsible to the library director, must assume authority for the library's display and exhibit program even though that person may not be directly involved with the hands-on operation. The individual must oversee the budgeting, planning, publicity and removal of all displays and exhibits.

Exhibit Costs

The costs for exhibits can present a problem to libraries during this period of tight money. If possible, a separate line in the library's public relations budget should be set aside for displays and exhibits. Although the initial capital expense for bulletin boards, display cases, lights and materials can be raised through general funds or a special gift, maintenance of an ongoing program will require additional expenditure. For an exhibit that requires special lighting or materials it is possible to obtain a gift from a member of the community or Friends; the donor may be honored with a small card beside or within the exhibit case stating that the exhibit is made possible through the generosity of the donor. This courtesy may also lead to additional gifts or suggestions of other exhibits supported by an individual patron.

Insurance

In some cases it may be necessary to obtain outside insurance to protect property that has been loaned to the library. If an individual asks the library to assume full responsibility for the safety of a collection that has significant value, the library director should be informed. In many cases, insurance currently held by the town or library itself may cover a valuable collection. A close examination of the policy will reveal the extent of the library's coverage. If additional coverage is required, contact the government official or department responsible for the municipality's insurance needs before shopping around. A short-term policy covering a specific exhibit is obtainable at a reasonable cost.

It is important, however, to determine the value of an exhibit. This is not always easy to do. In some cases an exhibit has been over-valued by the lender and the estimate may not be honored by an insurance company following loss. Whenever possible, require the lender to obtain an independent appraisal that will be honored by an insurance company.

Security Systems

Another precaution that can be considered is the use of a security device to protect the display from theft. Special devices are available to protect exhibit cases from being entered or pictures and paintings from being removed from a wall. These devices range from sophisticated electronic systems with auxiliary battery-powered back-up systems to rather simple battery-operated hardware that will ring an alarm if a glass case is broken, opened or moved. Electric eyes are available which will sound an alarm if anyone enters a room after hours. Motion detectors are so sensitive today that a strong wind passing through an "armed" room will set off the alarm.

The Yellow Pages lists local companies that sell security equipment. If there is a museum near the library, you might discuss security equipment with the director. Often special devices used in museums may be loaned to a library for a brief period. Because of the special nature of most museum security equipment, a local merchant may not have the specific items required for your needs.

LIBRARY PROGRAMS

One of the most popular methods of using library facilities to serve the community and promote the library is to develop a variety of programming activities. These activities can range from a children's movie to a musical event to a lecture series arranged in conjunction with a community group. There is hardly a public library in the country that has not developed a reading program for children. The most universal have been the story-oriented programs for preschoolers or the more formal story hours for older children.

The concept of a story hour has expanded in many parts of the country to include additional programs for young people. In New Jersey, for example, libraries have produced kite flying programs, a talking bird show, a series of lecture-demonstrations, and a hobby-swap-shop. These programs have proved to be immensely popular with the young people in their communities. At a New Jersey State Library-sponsored workshop on young adult services, a meeting that brought some 30 teenagers and approximately 75 library directors and their young adult specialists together, "the idea was expressed again and again that the youngsters ought to be formally involved in the planning of all library activities. There ought to be a Teen Program Committee, with the teens themselves the principal members; the kids should be represented on a Materials Selection Committee; and even, as is the case with at least one New Jersey library, be a member of the Board of Trustees of the library."[3]

Programs should not, of course, be limited to children's interests. There is a growing use of library facilities for a multitude of programs appealing to all segments of a community. The type of programs that a library can produce is partly dependent on budgetary considerations. Unless the library is sure that it can recoup its investment in a speaker or performer by charging an admission fee at the door, it is better to leave the business of producing a "big name event" to those who can afford to take a gamble. If a local organization is available to guarantee the library's investment, such an "event" may be worth considering.

PUBLIC SPEAKERS

Obtaining a public speaker need not be expensive and is, perhaps, the easiest type of program to offer. In many cases speakers are available at no charge, and the costs to a library to produce a lecture rarely exceed the cost of publicizing the event plus minor housekeeping costs.

Finding Local Talent

Locating speakers may require some imagination, and the community itself is the best place to start. A local industry can often provide an expert to share his or her knowledge with a library audience. Local utility companies have professional speakers on their staff—and on their payrolls—for public speaking engagements. Oil companies in particular have become extremely aware of their public image and have established a stable of speakers to meet with local groups. Obviously, any speaker from a special interest group will be "selling" the group's point of view. However, this should not rule out the use of such a speaker. If it's possible to arrange a public confrontation between advocates of two opposing viewpoints a far more exciting and interesting program will result.

Local merchants may provide speakers on their specialties. The wine merchant may sponsor an exhibit and lecture on wine with an accompanying wine and cheese tasting session; an antiques store owner can be called on to exhibit and speak on collecting; the golf club might send the club pro to speak about equipment and technique. The possibilities are endless.

Locating interesting speakers from within the community can be accomplished through a village survey. A questionnaire distributed at the circulation desk or mailed to community members can provide much useful information. In her article, "P.P. & P.R. Two Keys to Circulation Success," Marcia Posner describes what happened to one librarian who discovered through a library survey that the community contained a large, "hidden" Italian population:

> Alerted to the existence of the Italian Americans, the well-intentioned librarian hastened to make up for lost time. Soon the entire community was knee-deep in Italian culture: the library held musicales of opera recordings with librettos; poetry, art, and crafts sessions and of course, pasta parties. While the Italian patrons twirled and dipped to the strains of the tarantella with their indigenous neighbors, who immediately signed up as library patrons, five Indian families recently arrived from Pakistan walked in, attracted by the green, white and red banner fluttering outside the library door. As she welcomed them, the now sensitized librarian envisioned an Indian Festival.[4]

The questionnaire will reveal not only the specialties of many community members and hence their potential areas of expertise, but the broad interests of the community as well. Is there a desire for a lecture series on home repair? Cooking? Financial planning?

Speakers are also available from schools and local colleges, often for a nominal honorarium or as a public service. Other sources of expertise may be found through local, county, city, state or federal government agencies. A check of the various government organization manuals should lead to individuals in your area. In addition, the local phone directory should be a resource of prime importance.

Visiting Lecturers

Speakers from out of town may be a bit harder to find but may be worth pursuing. As noted previously, both local and national book and magazine publishers may be contacted for author-speakers. Author tours are now commonplace. Although most of these tours tend to bring a notable author before the media in large cities, it is possible for a library to take advantage of a break in an author's schedule and arrange for an appearance in a smaller community.

Speakers obtained from the "lecture circuit" are far more easily obtainable; however, there is a fee involved. Professional speakers' bureaus supply lists of their lecturers. Usually, prices are not contained in the agency's literature. In almost all cases fees are negotiable. The fee for a major international figure may climb well above $10,000 plus expenses for a single lecture. For an author with a national reputation fees can range from $1,000 and up. Quite often it is possible to "make a deal" with an agency to obtain a speaker if he or she happens to be speaking elsewhere in your area. Since most speakers are booked for a specific date far in advance, it becomes advantageous for both speaker and agency to book as many engagements as possible in a region for an individual on tour. If the library is able to adjust its schedule to the availability of a speaker, a substantial price reduction can be achieved. In addition to a fee, usually paid directly to the agency, travel, lodging and food expenses are also paid by the library. Lecture bureaus that have worked with libraries include:

ALA The Latin American Lecture Bureau
2355 Salzedo St., Suite 203
Coral Gables, FL 33134
305-442-2462

American Program Bureau
850 Boylston St.
Chestnut Hill, MA 02167
617-731-0500

Royce Carlton, Inc.
866 United Nations Plaza
New York, NY 10017
212-355-3210

Richard Fulton, Inc.
850 Seventh Ave.
New York, NY 10019
212-582-4099

Keedick Lecture Bureau, Inc.
475 Fifth Ave.
New York, NY 10017
212-683-5627

W. Colston Leigh, Inc.
49-51 State Rd.
Princeton, NJ 08540
609-921-6141

Public Affairs Lecture Bureau
104 E. 40th St.
New York, NY 10016
212-986-4456

Viewpoint Speakers Bureau
410 West St.
New York, NY 10014
212-242-7654

Visiting lecturers do require some care and handling. A person coming into your city for the first time will usually expect the sponsor (the library) to make arrangements for room reservations and meals. If an outside organization is working with the library, particularly if it is funding the lecturer, a dinner or reception is often in order. Like the lecture, these additional arrangements require coordination and planning. If the lecturer is an author, has the local book store been notified to plan a special exhibit of the individual's latest book? Is there an exhibit in the library of the person's works?

Funding a single lecture or lecture series can present problems. Again, local business and industry can be called upon for assistance. Banks, real estate companies, insurance companies, stock brokers and department stores are all potential sponsors. A major department store may well work with the library in not only funding but supplying decorations, food or professional guidance in planning a large program.

MOTION PICTURES

Films for young people and the Saturday cartoon festival used to be standard library fare before the advent of Captain Kangaroo and a Saturday morning filled with cartoons on every TV channel. Although films for young people have diminished in popularity, movies are far from a dead entertainment vehicle in the library.

There are several problems with film showings, however. It is difficult to obtain desirable films without charge. Although many library systems and state library film archives do have films that are available without cost, for the most part these are documentary in nature or not attractive to a wide audience. Keep in mind that any program sponsored by the library will compete with television programs as well as other local events scheduled when you are showing your film.

Film rental agencies do provide fine films, many of recent vintage. The rental cost will vary with the film as well as the purpose of the exhibitor. If the library is planning to charge an admission fee, the rental agency will usually expect a substantial royalty based upon door receipts. The royalty can be as high as 50% of gross revenues with a guaranteed minimum. A contract must be signed and the library is responsible for all delivery costs plus any charges that may be incurred if the film is damaged during the showing.

If, on the other hand, the library wants to rent a film and not charge an admission fee, there is a flat fee for a one-time showing. This fee can range from $35 for an older classic to $300-$500 for a recent release. Cartoons, shorts, serials, previews of coming attractions and documentaries are all available from a rental agency for a small fee.

One restriction that is placed upon libraries and other nonprofit groups that rent a film for free showing prevents the public promotion or advertising of the film. This caveat does not prevent the library from announcing the film showing with posters or notices in the library or a news release in the press. (See Figure 3.2.) It does preclude a paid ad in the newspaper, the spreading of posters in the community, or the publication of the film's name. Although this non-advertising agreement and a ''one-time use'' agreement is written into most contracts that the library must sign, it is possible to have this agreement waived under some circumstances. One Friends of the Library group produced a film festival of ''Oldies but Goodies'' for the community. Although the contract they had to sign did preclude them from showing a film more than once and announcing the film outside the library, the Friends contacted the rental agency and requested permission to show a film to an adult audience on a Monday evening and to a student group the next afternoon. They also asked if they could put posters up in the local schools. The response they received from the agency was, ''Well, you're not supposed to do it, but since we don't know about it who's to complain?''

The cost of film rental, like the cost to ''rent'' a speaker, is also negotiable. Although there is very little room to negotiate when renting one film, the library that plans a series and agrees to rent all films from a single source has a strong negotiating position. Don't be afraid to say that your budget won't allow you to acquire a certain film at the price listed in the catalog. The identical film may be carried by many film rental agencies, so shop around.

Figure 3.2   Library Film Series Publicized in a Friends' Newsletter

FRIENDS OF THE SCARSDALE LIBRARY

Editor — **William E. Penny**   *Acting Library Director*—**Virginia Barnett**

Issue Number 37   BOOKMARKS   July/August 1981

SUMMER FILM SERIES

The Friends of the Library have selected five films for their third annual summer film festival. The films, which are free and open to the public, will be shown in the Library's Scott Room at 8:00 p.m. on consecutive Tuesday evenings.

July 21 — *Mash*

A witty and funny movie, directed by Robert Altman, which won an Oscar for Best Screenplay and which has become a popular TV series. Set during the Korean War, the crew of surgical unit MASH 4077 clown and pull outrageous pranks to offset the horrors of war. Actors include Donald Sutherland, Elliot Gould, Sally Kellerman, Robert Duvall, Tom Skerritt, and Gary Burghoff.

July 28 — *The Seven Year Itch*

When a New York publisher's wife goes away for the long, hot summer, he finds himself succumbing to forbidden liquor, cigarettes, and dreams of girls — especially the well-stacked blonde upstairs who almost promises but never delivers. Directed by Billy Wilder and starring Marilyn Monroe and Tom Ewell.

Army nurse Lt. Dish (Jo Ann Pflug) detects understandable heart flutter in Trapper John (Elliot Gould) in *Mash*. Credit: Cinemabilia, Inc.

Greta Garbo and John Barrymore in a scene from *Grand Hotel*. Credit: Cinemabilia, Inc.

August 4 — *The Thin Man*

With characters based on his real-life relationship with Lillian Hellman, Dashiell Hammett's *The Thin Man* has emerged as a detective genre masterpiece. William Powell and Myrna Loy are delightful as the couple who drink cocktails, solve murders, and exchange insolent remarks with pleasure.

August 11 — *Grand Hotel*

An Oscar-winning, star-studded extravaganza, *Grand Hotel's* greatest guest is luminous Greta Garbo as a Russian ballerina who falls in love with jewel thief John Barrymore. A young, sexy, and irresistible Joan Crawford plays secretary to uncouth Wallace Berry in this classic drama.

August 18 — *The Hustler*

Paul Newman is Fast Eddie, a brash, cocky, itinerant pool shark who challenges top man Jackie Gleason for the championship. In his desperation, he sacrifices everything to win until he realizes the stakes are too high. Newman's dynamic performance is matched by George C. Scott's as an unscrupulous gambler.

Source: Scarsdale (NY) Public Library.

Certain films may be unavailable for rental, particularly if a film company is planning to rerelease a motion picture. Walt Disney films are constantly rereleased and the films are often restricted.

Names and addresses of local film rental agencies can be found in *Audio Visual Market Place* (R.R. Bowker Co., New York, NY). Certain agencies carry only foreign films; others carry the broad spectrum of classics and contemporary films.

BOOK CLUBS

Another growing trend in libraries is the organization of book clubs or reading groups centered around a central theme. Senior citizens, in particular, have been attracted to library book clubs that offer the opportunity for intellectual stimulation and the chance to meet new friends. In general, a librarian or community volunteer is chosen to lead the group. Usually a central theme is selected and a series of books is picked on the basis of their relationship to the theme. Members of the club or group either borrow the books from the library or obtain their own copies from a local book store. Discussions are held at the library on a periodic basis.

One organization, the Great Books Foundation (307 North Michigan Ave., Chicago, IL 60601), has a formal program for library book discussion groups. The organization, which was founded at the University of Chicago in 1947, has more than 265,000 members today. For a fee of $28 the Foundation trains a library staff member, or any other community member, during two half-day sessions. The sessons are held throughout the country and are usually easily accessible. Session leaders are taught how to organize courses under the guidance of the Foundation, how to select themes of popular interest to a community and how to conduct the sessions. The basic principal of the Foundation is to stimulate individual thinking. There is no single point of view, and leaders are taught to ask stimulating questions that may have a variety of answers. Librarians may attend sessions in either Great Books or Junior Great Books depending upon the desired audience.

Once the program is implemented no fee is charged by the library or the Foundation to members of the community attending the sessions. The only cost is acquiring the books. The Foundation does sell paperbound copies of books for their programs; however, the books may be easily obtained at the library or book store. There are 16 sessions for each series with the number of books required for a series varying depending on the series. A series on plays or short stories may require more books than a series on the novel. Usually the Foundation will provide the books needed for a single series at a cost of $15.

DISCUSSION GROUPS

Library discussion groups are similar in concept to the book club, except that the topics for discussion are not related to a series of books. For example, a local United Nations group may sponsor a discussion on peace in the Middle East. The group, in cooperation with the library, produces a bibliography of related books and articles. The group also provides a speaker or discussion leader at each session. A debate between individuals representing opposing points of view may open a session. The following discussion then focuses on the points raised during the debate. Guest speakers may be called upon to present a point of view, then moderate the discussion that follows. Although community issues are important subjects for discussion, such national and international topics as politics, morality, freedom of the press, education, health and medicine, crime and justice, etc. are more likely to stimulate opposing viewpoints.

The library's role in organizing a program or group discussion is purely to supply the facility where people can meet and obtain information. Unless the topic is related directly to the library, the library should not be stating a point of view. Obviously staff members must be free to attend a discussion group meeting and state their own beliefs. It must be clear, however, that the opinions of any library employee do not represent the position or policy of the library.

MUSICAL EVENTS

Not all libraries have the facilities to program events requiring live music. (Obviously, lectures or discussions involving records present little problem.) Since a piano is often the mainstay of a musical program both space and cost may preclude this form of public presentation.

If it is possible to present popular or classical musical programs, the library is an excellent place to hold the event. Often local schools and colleges are focal points for musical programs, but it is often possible to hold a student concert in the library. In many communities a concert held in a school will draw primarily the family, friends and relatives of the performers. A musical program in the library stands a far greater chance of involving more community members.

In addition to the local public schools, special music schools in the area may be a source of musical talent for the library program director. Talent agencies exist for those who are interested in booking the services of professional musicians. The cost of a musician or musical group will range from a few hundred dollars to many thousands. Top professionals can obtain fees as high as $40,000 per performance. Many groups, particularly popular music groups, also expect a portion of gross receipts.

TRIPS

Although the library is not in the business of operating a travel agency, opportunities do arise in which the library can blend its resources with the wanderlust of many of its patrons. In addition to displays of travel books and literature that can enhance a special exhibit, special bibliographies can be prepared and distributed in conjunction with a travel-related show.

Arrangements can also be made with a professional travel agency to coordinate a library exhibit, display and bibliography. For example, a local travel agent might plan a group trip to China in cooperation with a village organization or a local alumni association. The library can serve as a focal point by arranging, in conjunction with the groups, a lecture or series of lectures on China, a documentary film and a display of China-related objects. The library can also exhibit its collection of books and periodicals on China and prepare a more detailed bibliography of materials that would interest not only the potential travelers but the community at large.

There are trips that the library itself can sponsor. Although these are unlikely to involve foreign or exotic travel, they can be of significant value to the community. For example, walking tours within the community or a neighboring city can be extremely interesting, provided a capable tour leader is obtained. A walking tour, a visit to historic local homes or architectural sites, or simply a tour of a nearby historic landmark can be coordinated with the local historical society. If the community does not have an active historical group, contact the state historian and obtain names and addresses of individuals who are qualified to lead a group and who are familiar with the specific landmarks near your community.

When considering the library's travel program, think in the broadest terms. Is it possible to organize a group visit to a nearby theatrical event? Museum? Concert or opera? All these trips plus a host of others that may be unique to a specific library or community enhance the value of the library when properly planned, executed and coordinated with the library's complete resources.

PLAYS

Few libraries have the facilities for a major stage presentation. But lack of a stage, lighting devices and Broadway sets should not preclude a library from offering theater to the public. A simple play reading or a workshop production by talented amateurs can be most rewarding. Young people's groups can be encouraged to work with the library in presenting plays for the community or their peers.

If a dramatic production is planned by the library, it is important to clear the rights to the play with the copyright owner. There are several major companies that provide copies of plays that are not in the public domain as well as information concerning rights. French & Co. in New York City is, perhaps, the largest. In determining whether or not a play is in the public domain it is important to determine not only the date of the original publication but the date of the translation (if it is a non-English-language play). A play or translation published prior to 1906 is in the public domain. A play published later may or may not be in the public domain depending upon copyright renewal. If there is a doubt, a letter to the copyright office, Library of Congress, will elicit the information.

BOOK FAIRS

The book fair is gaining great popularity as a means to draw people to the library and to generate revenue. A book fair can be held under the auspices of either the library or a community group working with the library. Book fair organizers solicit book donations from the community and sell them at the fair together with many of the library's own books that have been weeded from the collection. In some communities the book fair also serves as a common display ground for other community groups to describe their activities to fair attendees or to generate income through the sale of items such as food, plants, raffle tickets, crafts, etc. The book fair is usually held either in the library or on the library grounds. However, if the fair is part of a major community fundraising activity, there is no reason why the book fair has to be held on library property.

Organization of a book fair will vary. Some libraries use a series of small booths within the library, each booth selling a particular type of book. Other libraries, primarily in suburban and rural areas, may set up outdoor tables. An outdoor fair does present a potential problem during inclement weather. Thus, either an alternative "rain date" must be selected or the library must have a contingency plan to move the fair indoors.

Organizing the Fair

Organization of the actual event usually becomes the responsibility of the library director. However, because of the large amount of work involved in coordinating all activities the director usually assigns to a staff member or volunteer the job of putting all the pieces together and running the fair. Often, the book fair is run by the Friends of the Library in cooperation with the library staff. Regardless of who has the ultimate responsibility for planning and putting on a book fair, it is a major operation that can be of significant benefit to the library if done well.

Careful and early consideration must be given to selecting a date for the fair. Obviously, an outdoor fair in the winter is out of the question for libraries not located in the Sun Belt. Conversely, an indoor fair held in an unairconditioned library on a hot summer's day will not entice many customers. The Scarsdale Public Library holds its annual book fair in the fall. The date is chosen almost a year in advance. In choosing the date there are two primary considerations: the fair can't be held on a religious holiday, and it can't be held if another crowd-drawing event is scheduled. If, for example, the high school football team is to play a game away from home, that date is eliminated; experience has taught fair organizers that book fair attendance drops significantly when community members leave town to watch the game.

The library used to hold its annual fair on the library grounds, but unpredictable fall weather was a constant threat. Several years ago the fair was held in the library without a drop in attendance. The library also discovered another benefit to the indoor fair: incidence of book theft dropped considerably when the activity was moved inside.

Gathering and Sorting the Books

Obtaining books for the fair is another opportunity to involve the community in the work of the library. An announcement in the local paper and posters in the library that the library is to hold a book fair and needs books to sell can bring out a flood of attic cleaners laden with boxes. Unfortunately, a great many of these "gifts" will be unsaleable. Encyclopedias long out-of-date, books with torn pages, campaign biographies of politicians long passed into obscurity and 20-year-old professional books in fields undergoing constant change will beg for buyers. The receiver, however, can't pick and choose what books may be donated to the fair. What usually happens is that many "gifts" end up in a rubbish heap. However, in with the potential discards will be many books, often gems, that will appeal to fair goers.

Since many book donors are using their gift to the library as a tax deduction, the library may be asked to provide a receipt for donated books. It is always good public relations to write a personal letter to the donor thanking the individual or family for the gift, but the library must not try to place a value on the books. The library is not in a position to provide an accurate assessment of used books and would not want its letter to be used by the donor to establish the value of the gift to the Internal Revenue Service. A letter simply stating that the library thanks the donor for the thoughtful gift of X number of books will suffice.

Sorting the books prior to sale is another job that must be carefully organized. The simplest method is to cull all unwanted books first. With the books that are to be sold establish simple categories: reference, mysteries, how-to books, travel, fiction, cookbooks, etc. The paperbacks can be segregated and sold at a set price per title. To separate all paper-back books into categories can be a very time-consuming activity.

Pricing

In the late 1970s a book fair sponsored by a large college alumni association accepted 50 cents for a rare book that later sold for several hundred dollars. This, of course, is the exception. However, there is little question that a well run book fair will present a great many bargains for the careful buyer.

Pricing the books is perhaps the most difficult decision that fair organizers must make. There is no hard and fast rule. However, there are a few guidelines. As mentioned, if all paperback books are sold for one price it makes both shopping and collecting payment much easier. Reference books can usually bear a higher price. Books in poor condition will have to be priced accordingly. Since the object of the book fair is to raise money for the library and, at the same time, provide some book bargains for the community, pricing must not be so high that dissatisfied customers result. It is better to sell books for less money than have a bad public image. Also, it helps to sell as many books as possible. Unlike a book store, the library can't return unsold books.

Another method to move books is to announce that several hours before the end of the book fair all remaining unsold books will be discounted 10% or 20%. An hour before clos-ing, books can be discounted 50%. Be assured that the best books will sell fast and first. In fact, many book fairs have been known to attract a bevy of used-book dealers who will be the first in line to buy books. They will buy hundreds of volumes to stock their own stores. These same books will then be marked up several hundred percent.

Special Sale Items

Some libraries sell other items at a book fair. Cider and donuts in the fall and plants in the spring can serve to generate additional revenue. In addition to selling books, the book fair is an excellent opportunity to show off the library. If there is a new service available, a display or announcement can be made at the fair. Librarians, usually seen in their more formal role, can talk more casually with fair attendees and, perhaps, recommend specific books of interest.

The silent auction is another way to generate interest and revenue at the book fair. If the library has received books of more than passing interest or value they should be able to command a higher price. Books or other highly saleable objects can be displayed several weeks before the book fair. Each item is described and patrons are invited to place a sealed bid for an item or two in a locked box. At the close of the book fair the box is opened and the individual bidding the highest price for an item receives it.

What To Do with the Leftovers

Disposing of unsold books is another problem facing the book fair organizers. In some cases books may be held over until the next fair. However, if the book didn't sell at one book fair its chances of being sold the next time around will be fairly slim. It's better to donate unsold books to another institution than to hold them over until the next fair. Hospitals, schools, prisons, senior citizens' homes, veterans' organizations and military base libraries should be considered as possible recipients of unsold books. In many cases, unfortunately, the book may simply have to be discarded.

Benefits of the Fair

A library book fair requires a great deal of work. The results, however, can be extremely rewarding. Not only will the library benefit financially, but the interest of the community is focused upon the library as a positive community force. The many staff members and volunteer workers share the pleasure of seeing their efforts come to fruition. A book fair can bring together many elements of the community—teenagers and seniors, library staff members and community volunteers.

PUBLICIZING SPECIAL EVENTS

Special exhibits and programs require special publicity efforts. The worst sentence a program planner can hear from a patron is, "I didn't know you were doing that." In addition to posters in the library and throughout the community, a formal press release should be issued well before any program. A major event should be publicized with a series of press announcements to the media. In some cases, an important lecturer for example, a press release describing the event as a "news item" and a background story on the speaker or event should also be issued. Although a release following an event may seem like an afterthought to some, it has the value of establishing the library as an arena where news is made.

If the program is one that should be photographed, as either part of a news story or for archival records, it is the responsibility of the program coordinator to assign a photographer to the event. In many instances the local paper will send a photographer, if requested; however you may need to make a few follow-up phone calls to the paper as reminders.

Some programs should be recorded on audio or video tape. A special lecture, musical event, poetry reading, play, etc. can be taped and stored for future listening or viewing. These recordings should be cataloged and promoted for the entire community to share. In communities with cable television outlets, it is sometimes possible to have the cable firm tape a library program for showing throughout the cable system's network.

Libraries that present many programs often issue a special calendar listing dates and events. This schedule is distributed to the community at the library and is given to local merchants and the media. A library's calendar of events can also be mailed to patrons together with other items of library news. Highlights, of course, should be part of a newsletter. There can never be too much publicity. And, regardless of how much you try to get the message across, you can be assured that there will always be a segment of the community that never gets the message.

READING LISTS AND BIBLIOGRAPHIES

A special library service that engenders good will is the development of a list or bibliography of selected books, articles, AV materials, motion pictures and even, if possible, computer software for different segments of the library's audience. The purpose of a current list is simply to have on hand the answer to the question a patron may ask, "Do you have any information on . . .?" In addition, a properly conceived bibliography should encourage individuals to go beyond the card catalog in searching for information, that is, to use the library's fullest resources.

A bibliography must be kept up to date and must be called to the attention of library patrons. The areas of coverage are as varied as the numbers in the Dewey decimal system. There are, however, some basic areas that library patrons will want to know about. Although the broad areas of interest will also vary with the library and the library's users, the basics should include lists of materials on consumerism, cooking, travel, taxes, gardening, child care, and various fields of business, science and technology. Additional lists could easily subdivide the basics. For example, a list of basic cookbooks could also include a section on specialty items, foods of different nations and, perhaps, a section on canning and preserving. The list should cover books currently available, journal articles (for journals held by the library), government publications, sections in reference materials that can be photocopied and any nonprint materials that the library may have available.

In addition to a collection of basic bibliographies, the library should strive to generate its own reading lists based on current interests, needs and events. For example, when the television program "Roots" became popular many libraries produced bibliographies on genealogy; the TV series on the Holocaust led to book lists about that subject. Even a popular motion picture like "Star Wars" could encourage a librarian to assemble a list of books devoted to science fiction and space facts.

Some current events may require the reading list to include more articles than books— for instance, the Iranian hostage crisis, reports of a medical breakthrough, an election, etc. This may mean culling through the current periodical reference guides to assemble a listing of pertinent articles. For the library fortunate enough to have access to an online biblio-graphic data base, the job of assembling a current listing becomes easier. However, be sure to check the references you obtain against your library's holdings. The fact that your library may not have all the items available is no reason not to include an important reference. However, if a particular book or article is not available at the library be sure to note this fact on the reading list. By checking with a county, system, state or school union catalog it is possible to identify the locations of an item not in the library. These locations should then be mentioned in the reading list.

Sources of Bibliographies

The federal government produces many bibliographies on a wide variety of subjects. Listings of materials published or distributed by the U.S. Government Printing Office are available for the asking. Although the library will probably not own all items on the list, it can tell patrons where to obtain a particular item. The patron should be told that a govern-ment publication is available at many locations and not just through the Government Print-ing Office's Washington address. Regional distribution locations may be a short trip from a library. Often, patrons can get government documents at no cost through their U.S. Repre-sentative.

Libraries can obtain bibliographies and reading lists from the Library of Congress and the National Archives as well as a great many other federal agencies. These bibliographies are kept up to date and list books and articles published by both government and commer-cial publishers.

Another source of free bibliographies and reading lists is any of the thousands of pro-fessional and trade associations established to promote information about their own special interest. These can be extremely valuable lists; however, the user should be made aware that the group's own point of view will be highlighted in the bibliography. Naturally, one of the best groups to contact for current bibliographies is the American Library Association (50 E. Huron St., Chicago, IL 60611). For books dealing with specialized subjects such as busi-ness, art, political science, etc., try the Special Libraries Association (235 Park Ave. South, New York, NY 10003).

Preparing a List

Although the library director is responsible for developing an ongoing program to pro-duce bibliographies and reading lists, the actual preparation of the lists usually is assigned to either a reference librarian or a subject specialist. Lists of children's books, for example, will be prepared by the children's librarian. It is also possible to share the responsibility between library departments. The planning and assigning of book lists can be handled at general staff meetings. Since the bibliography has a strong impact upon the library's public relations ef-fort, the individual in charge of library PR should be directly involved in the planning stage.

In most cases the bibliography will need updating within a year. In some cases, lists will require revision more often. Thus, printing large quantities of a bibliography is probably unwise, as well as expensive. There is no reason why an attractive mimeographed list can't be produced fairly inexpensively. By mimeographing on both sides of a standard 8½- by 11-inch sheet of paper you will have more room for an attractive design element, and the bibliography can be folded to make a 4¼- by 11-inch flyer.

It is possible to enlist the cooperation of a local business in funding a book list. For example, a list of publications on estate planning, income taxes, investing, etc. could be funded by a community bank. The bibliography might then be printed (at the bank's expense) with a statement thanking the bank for making the bibliography available to the community. When a business provides financial support for a published bibliography, the business will also want to have a supply available for distribution to its own customers.

Distribution

The distribution of any book list should go beyond the library if at all possible. Certainly, there should be a cooperative arrangement between libraries in the same community or neighboring communities. The good idea your library may have for a bibliography may be repaid many times over by good ideas from other area libraries.

If the bibliography is related to a local business, then another outlet is available for distribution. For example, a list of travel books should be made available to travel agents; books on money matters should be shared with banks, stock brokers and insurance companies; books, articles or pamphlets on cooking and food preparation could be placed on the checkout counters of local supermarkets.

It pays to do a little market research on your own to determine whether or not your lists are actually being circulated outside the library. Ask patrons if they have seen your lists. If so, where? Most important, have the lists been of value to the library's patrons? Ask the circulation desk librarians if they are aware of any circulation trends for particular books following the distribution of a bibliography on a certain subject.

If space is available on a bibliography, try providing library patrons with a check list of suggested areas in which new book lists can be prepared. Also ask for specific suggestions for additional bibliographies. And by all means take advantage of the bibliographies that are being circulated to call the reader's attention to other lists available at the library.

Occasionally the local newspaper might mention the availability of a new bibliography. Certainly if the library is planning to produce a list that is tied to a community event, e.g., anniversary, local scout week, opening of a new business, etc., mention of the list could well accompany the write-up of the event that the paper is preparing.

CONCLUSION

Exhibits, special programs, book fairs and targeted reading lists are all ways to convince the community that the library is a full source of information and enjoyable experiences. All these activities require hard work, organization and leadership. The library director is ultimately responsible for ensuring that plans are well conceived, publicized and implemented. The cooperation of staff and volunteers is essential to success. Equally crucial is the development of a continuing positive relationship with the community at large. This is the subject of the next chapter.

FOOTNOTES

1. "Prepare: The Library Public Relations Recipe Book," mimeographed (Preconference publication of the Public Relations Section, Library Administration Division, American Library Association, 1978), p. 34.

2. Marie D. Loizeaux, *Publicity Primer* (New York: H.W. Wilson Co, 1959), p. 54.

3. Marya Hunsicker, "Public Relations in a Children's Room," in *Public Relations for Libraries,* ed. Allan Angoff (Westport, CT: Greenwood Press, 1973), p. 127.

4. Marcia Posner, "P.P. & P.R. Two Keys to Circulation Success," *SLJ School Library Journal* 22 (February 1976): 15.

4

Developing and Maintaining Community Relations

Because libraries must depend on the support of others for their existence, it is important—if not essential to survival—for them to understand and maintain a solid relationship with the local "power structure." In most communities library funding comes from tax monies; thus residents must be convinced that the library is as important an investment as any other community operation dependent on tax revenues. Unlike attendance at public schools, library attendance is not mandated by the state. Therefore, the library's budget is perhaps one of the easiest to compromise at budget-cutting time.

Moreover, while teachers, sanitation workers, police and fire department employees are usually protected to some extent by strong unions, librarians haven't produced a strong, national or local bargaining agent. If a strong library union did emerge, its position would probably be fragile. A community cannot survive long with a teacher, police, sanitation or fire department strike. Tragically, a community could tolerate a public librarians' strike for quite a long time. Since librarians lack the power to strike, they must rely on persuasion. They must work with political leaders, organizations and a broad range of citizens to ensure recognition of the library as an essential element in the life and future of the community.

Since the Boards of Trustees of public libraries are either elected by the community or appointed by the local government, there is a strong element of accountability. Obviously, if the Board does not operate the library in the community's best interest the Board can be replaced. This is not to suggest that an aura of partisan politics should exist. On the contrary, the library Board should be politically independent, serving only the community's needs.

LIAISON WITH GOVERNMENT

It is essential to determine which government officials are directly responsible for library activities. This certainly is not a difficult chore. Does the mayor have this responsibility? Is the mayor elected or appointed by a board? Is there a village manager who really controls the purse strings? Does the public library receive financial support from county or state sources? If so, who controls these funds? Is there a state library commissioner? Does this office exert financial influence or control over local funds? Does the state have a legislative committee on library activities? Who chairs this committee? Is he or she pro-library?

These questions may appear to be academic, but they directly affect the future of a library. Both the library director and the individual responsible for public relations should know the answers.

Working with Local Officials

Most important is the liaison with local government. This relationship is a two-way street. Not only should the village or city official be kept informed about library matters, but the library must also have an inside track on government plans and programs that may affect the library. It is the responsibility of the library director to establish and maintain this ongoing liaison. Unfortunately, pride can stand in the way of a productive relationship. If the village manager is responsible for library matters he or she will expect to deal with a library official of equal "rank." If the director delegates the liaison responsibility to a staff member the village official may feel slighted and may not respond to the library's needs. This may seem like a minor point, and it certainly is petty, yet the future of the library may suffer as a result.

The library director should establish a plan of operation in dealing with key local officials. The director and/or public relations person should attend board meetings, important committee meetings and major town events. Be visible! Make yourself known! Every government needs information. During labor negotiations, for example, it's important to have an ongoing file of salary schedules of comparable positions in the area. Other financial and general business data are constantly needed for government operations. By becoming the central information resource of the local government, the library gains not only visibility but becomes a necessary element in administering community affairs.

Although the director should make the initial contact and maintain the ongoing liaison with officials, it is important to delegate many of the information-gathering chores. If the town establishes a committee to do research on a particular topic, the library director might suggest that a library staff member serve on the committee as either a working member or a staff aid. This added work imposed upon a staff member must be compensated for in some manner. Don't expect staff librarians to volunteer for added responsibilities; they are usually overworked as it is. However, the value and importance of involving library personnel in the day-to-day operation of the local government is considerable.

Confidentiality and Impartiality

In addition to serving as a government information resource, the librarian must assure government officials that a confidential relationship can exist providing it doesn't violate "sunshine laws" requiring free access to public information. A village manager's request for information may relate to such confidential matters as staff problems, union negotiations or budgetary proposals. Here the library director must exercise discretion to protect the important ongoing relationship with village officials without negating the library's responsibility to be an impartial source of information.

A confidential request from a union or professional association for information must be treated in the same fashion as the request from the village official. In fact, it is highly probable that, during labor negotiations, both sides may request the identical data from the library. It becomes critical for the library to be an impartial servant to all members of the community. To favor one faction over another places the library in a delicate and dangerous political position. Like Switzerland, the library is neutral and can be a meeting ground for all political positions within a community.

Little Services that Matter

Harold L. Roth, former president of the New Jersey Library Association and Director of the Nassau County (NY) Reference Library, writes succinctly of library-government relations, particularly when the library is a new institution in a community:

> Each government tends to have its own method of action. . . . A new agency must fit itself into a pattern and watch the opportunities made available to it to move forward and make "Brownie points." . . . By asking questions properly, one moves ahead. By reacting properly to answers, one moves further ahead.
> Movement ahead is something so trivial as telling the county executive's secretary where to get a certain travel magazine. The contact rendered through as simple a service as that facilitates easy access to the county executive's office and smooths the way for contact with other executives there. Suddenly the library is put on the routing list for releases from that office, receives minutes of the Board of Supervisors, and is invited to special county functions. *The best part is a tacit agreement that requests to the county executive's office will not be conveniently lost, but will be passed on for effective action.*[1] (Italics added.)

A simple device is to post a list of local officials near library staff telephones, so that an individual who calls the library will be recognized by name. This courtesy may mean the difference between getting the next budget through the local city council or not.

OTHER COMMUNITY GROUPS

The relationship between library and government must not be the only community liaison. Every community has its share of public interest groups, such as garden clubs, womens' and mens' clubs, adult schools, neighborhood associations or trade unions. There are also local associations that play an active role in the governing and operation of a community, e.g., political parties, chambers of commerce, legal associations, etc. A relationship should be established with these power groups as well as with the actual governing body. This is not to suggest that a separate individual be named as a "liaison officer" to each group. However, meetings between the library director and group president or official should be held.

The purpose of a meeting is to assure each group that the public library serves all members of a community and welcomes the opportunity to work with groups to provide the full range of library services. If the library has a program or meeting room, a coordinated activity including a group special meeting and a library display or book list can be planned. The emphasis is on cooperation. The library has neither the time nor the resources to serve as a group's programming agent. However, the library can provide the information back-up to any activity that serves the general community interest.

FRIENDS OF THE LIBRARY

One of the most important groups in a library's marketing effort is the Friends of the Library. The ways various Friends' groups work with libraries vary quite widely. In some communities the Friends are primarily a fundraising group; in others they are an active part of the library's operations.

Membership in the Friends can be an expensive, exclusive "honor" or open to all who show an interest and fill out a membership card. Many Friends' groups have several membership options. For a few dollars the contributor can be a member; for $25, a contributing member; for $50, a sustaining member; $100, a patron; $500+, a lifetime patron, etc. Unless the Friends can afford to limit membership by making it expensive, it best serves the library's interest to have as broad a membership base as possible. After all, every individual who pays to join a Friends' group has clearly expressed a strong interest in the library and its operations.

Independent vs. Library-Operated Groups

Whereas most Friends are totally independent of library control, a few are organized and operated by the library itself. There are advantages and disadvantages to the library in both methods. An independent group can act without being tied to policy established by the library's Board of Trustees. Although there are few instances when the Friends will operate in opposition to general library policy, it can happen. A library may be reluctant to spend public funds for a venture that cannot be assured of total public support. For example, it might be desirable to hire a speaker for a fundraising dinner. But if ticket sales fail to meet the total expenses of the dinner and speaker, the event loses money—public money. The Friends can often take the gamble and expose their own funds to a potential loss in return for a possible substantial gain to the library.

From the library's point of view, it can be better to have greater control over the Friends by running the organization directly under the aegis of the library itself. However, the lack of independence can inhibit the organization's growth and development. Also, if a Friends' group is under the direct control of the library's director there is little opportunity for volunteers to have a direct policy voice in the Friends' activities. A weak director can lead to a weak Friends, whereas a weak president or chairperson of a Friends' organization can be voted out of office by the group's members.

Some independent Friends of the Library are extremely popular in the community and often exert a significant influence on library policy. The Friends of the Greenwich (CT) Library, for example, actually own the library building and are extremely influential in formulating policy. Although the community of Greenwich supplies the funds for the library's general operations, the Friends work closely with the director and library staff in planning various activities.

The Friends of the Scarsdale (NY) Public Library are another example of an active, independent group of community volunteers. Through its fundraising activities in 1980 alone, the group contributed more than $13,000 to the library. For a community of less than 20,000 residents this represented a significant amount. The Friends of the Scarsdale Public Library are responsible for organizing the annual book fair, an activity that raises in excess of $2500 a year. The group also sponsors a series of free public events including movies, lectures and seminars. Its annual meeting has become a major attraction because it features speakers of nationwide prominence—among them William F. Buckley Jr., Chaim Potok, Alfred Kazin, E.L. Doctorow, Joseph Heller and the late Justice William O. Douglas.

The Friends' president attends all meetings of the library's Board of Trustees. In turn, the Board appoints a liaison to the Friends to assure a smooth relationship between the groups. Several cooperative ventures have been highly successful. In 1978 the Friends provided a grant of $5000 to the Board to test the feasibility of hiring a part-time library program director. The experiment worked, and the following year a part-time position was established by the Board and was funded by the library. Another successful undertaking was a 1979 Friends grant to the library to hire an outside consultant to review the collection and submit a report to the community. The evaluation assisted the library in its overall aquisition policy and the Friends in determining which specific books to give to the library to enhance weak subject collections.

Problems can ensue with an independent Friends group in the area of fund raising. There are many members of the community who donate a generous amount to the Friends each year under the valid assumption that the money is being spent directly by the library. Actually, the library has no control over any of the Friends' income. When the library itself plans a general community fundraising activity, an extremely close liaison has to be established with the Friends to assure that one fundraising effort doesn't impede the effort of the other to the disadvantage of both groups and the community.

Friends' Activities

The Friends are involved in far more than fund raising and producing programs. The Friends of the Chicago (IL) Public Library, for example, present an annual award to a library employee in recognition of exceptional service to the public. Not to slight staff members who are not directly involved with the public, the Friends also give an award for distinguished work in nonpublic areas. Library patrons are invited to fill out forms available in the library to nominate a librarian for the Friends' public award; fellow staff members nominate the recipient of the award to the librarian in nonpublic areas. Friends at other libraries honor library staff members by teas, luncheons, an annual Christmas party, etc.

As a general rule, Friends assist the library in areas where the library itself lacks the time, talent or funds. For example, Friends may help organize fundraising campaigns to purchase objects needed by the library such as a new record player, microform machine, special books, etc; work in the library doing typing, filing and essential clerical work that may relieve a librarian; coordinate an exhibit or program, etc. According to Lawrence V. Mott, former President, Friends of the Denver (CO) Public Library:

> There are two areas where definite dislikes are indicated by many Friends. These are fund raising and political contact in support of the library. The Friends feel that financial campaigns are not a field for them. If such a campaign is necessary, it should be a single drive not to be repeated for a long time; the best procedure would be to enlist the Friends as part of a larger fundraising organization. These objections do not apply to programs to obtain money for the Friends' own finances.[2]

Despite these reflections, Friends' groups throughout the country have been highly significant in fund raising for the library. When a bond is required for a building program it is not uncommon to find the Friends in the forefront of community leadership during the fund drive. In 1973, for example, the Friends of California Libraries, Sierra Madre, CA, issued an excellent *Extension Kit,* which devoted several pages to describing the how-to's of bond selling for libraries. Information regarding the Friends of California *Extension Kit,* which covers many other how-to's for Friends, can be obtained by contacting the group at PO Box 455, Sierra Madre, CA 91024.

Political action by the Friends may be one of the most important advantages the group can offer the library. Since it is often difficult, and in fact undesirable, for the library itself to be directly involved in politics, the Friends can represent the library's interests. Political action takes many forms. A representative of the Friends can attend a city government board meeting and speak in the library's behalf; the Friends can endorse a new library site; they can sponsor campaigns to influence legislators on library-related matters. Friends can be extremely active when it comes to mixing politics and dollars. Friends have appeared in countless state capitals button-holing legislators in an active, highly visible lobbying effort to obtain additional funding for libraries or, more recently, to prevent cuts in library funds. (More information on legislative lobbying is given later in this chapter.)

The Friends of the Dallas (TX) Public Library were essential to the success of the system's branch library expansion effort. Before starting on an active public campaign, the Friends hired a noted library consultant to survey the city's branch library needs. With the consultant's report in hand, the Friends next approached the city council with hard data that the city of Dallas did, indeed, need more branch libraries. Largely because of the Friends' efforts, the council included $1 million for a capital improvement program.

However, the Friends in Dallas weren't through. The branch libraries required a bond issue which had to be approved by the public. A list of all qualified voters in the precincts closest to the proposed branch sites was obtained. The president of the Friends then signed and mailed 46,000 post cards to those voters, urging them to go to the polls and vote "yes" on the ballot for branch libraries. The Friends then mailed 800 letters to the presidents of Dallas' leading clubs and organizations. A Friends-sponsored ad in the local newspaper urged support of the library bonds. Posters and special displays were assembled in the Dallas main library and the existing branch libraries showing architectural plans for the new branches plus the rationale for the necessary additional branches.

The effectiveness of the Friends' campaign became clear when the votes were counted. Not only did the library bonds carry by a wide margin, but they drew more favorable votes than any other proposition on the ballot, even though voters knew that approval would increase their taxes.

Another successful, though less obvious, political effort was mounted by the Friends of the Cornell Public Library (now the Tompkins County Public Library, Ithaca, NY). The group's activity "has never amounted to a political struggle between factions as in some cities. It has simply been a quiet and persistent pressure to make those responsible for the budget see that a library can be as important as a public park or a golf course, even perhaps as important as good roads and a police force."[3] The low-key operation of Ithaca's Friends paid off. In one decade the annual appropriation for the library increased fourfold.

Moving Beyond the Local Library

Friends need not, in fact should not, limit their attention to their own library. County and state libraries are important elements in the total library benefits members of any community receive, and they need Friends, too. There are a host of examples illustrating that Friends have played an important role in assisting the public library concept by working outside the immediate community. State libraries in Mississippi, North Dakota, Louisiana and Kentucky have benefited from state citizen movements. Says Mary B. Gray, who revived the organization of Friends of Kentucky Libraries and offered the first state-owned bookmobile to the first county which would consent to run it:

> There is a definite advantage to beginning the Friends work on a state-county setup rather than as separate groups of Friends of town libraries. Such a procedure obliges the town to include its rural neighbors in its activities. There is always the tendency for towns, even small ones, to think only of their own libraries and to confine themselves to the small group of people living close enough to meet easily. With telephones and a better transportation system there is no need for a gap between farm and town. Where there are two rival towns, tact is necessary to obtain cooperation, but given time and the incentive of state and federal aid it can be done."[4]

ORGANIZING A FRIENDS' GROUP

Organizing a Friends' group can be initiated by any individual or group with the interests of the library as a common focal point. In most cases there is a specific need which generates the incentive for an individual or group to take the initiative. This need is usually brought about by such conditions as budgetary problems, a new building or addition to the library, a wish to improve the book collection or, simply, the desire to promote public awareness of the library's services or problems. Often the impetus comes from the library director or staff; in any case, librarians should be aware of the mechanics of running a Friends' group.

Start-up

The initial task in starting a Friends' group is to assure that the organizers have the wherewithal to plan and implement the proposed project. An aborted attempt to organize a Friends of the Library will do disservice to the library. The financial aspect isn't critical during the early period of organization; dedication is! Before embarking on a plan, the organizers should meet with the director of the library as well as with a member of the Board of Trustees and the town official responsible for library operations. Although there is no need for a formal approval or "blessing" from these individuals, the success of future activities often hinges on the support and vocal approval of those formally involved with the library. In addition, since public relations is an ongoing part of the Friends' *raison d'*être, why not start at the beginning?

Next come the actual mechanics of organization and implementation. One method is to place notices in the village newspaper and in the library that a meeting is scheduled for a specific date to discuss the organization of a Friends of the Library. At the meeting, a temporary chairperson is selected and various committees are named to study and recommend a more formal organization with constitution and by-laws. In most cases, this method of organization boils down to a one- or two-person task. Usually, a large number of community residents will applaud the idea and provide a great deal of verbal support; however, finding dedicated workers from this throng can be frustrating. In most cases, a small group can handle the assignment with little difficulty. This core will probably consist of the individuals who conceived the idea of founding a Friends' group in the first place.

Often the initiative to organize a Friends' group is generated from an existing community organization. For example, the Jacksonville, FL, chapter of the American Association of University Women became interested in the city library, formed a steering committee and broadened its membership to include citizens representing library trustees, city officials, and various civic, cultural and educational organizations. From the steering committee came the genesis of the Friends of the Jacksonville Library.

Constitution or Charter

Several committees or sub-committees will work out the basic details that will determine the future of the Friends. The first question that must be addressed is the charter or constitution. A charter is a legal document, filed with the appropriate state court, and conforms to the laws of the state. If the group intends to acquire a substantial amount of property, a charter should be drafted. A constitution differs from a charter in that it is not filed with the state and is not an official public record. Most Friends opt for the constitution. Both, however, specify the following: name and purpose of organization, statement of membership qualifications, officers and their method and term of election, and methods of amending.

The constitution's by-laws contain the detailed rules and procedures of operation. Since the Friends will be collecting and spending money, it is important that the group register with the appropriate state body to obtain a nonprofit, tax-exempt status. A unique I.D. number will be issued and the organization is exempt from sales taxes on goods and services received. In addition, the organization can receive gift funds that may be exempted from state and federal income taxes.

The by-laws will establish the organizational structure of the group. In most cases, the Friends operate by means of committees. Aside from the basic committees involved in the organizational structure (nominating, constitution, etc.) separate committees are often selected to handle specific Friends' activities, e.g., fund raising, publicity or programming. Some Friends' groups establish a young people's Friends of the Library to teach young library users that library service is not reserved to librarians or older volunteers.

To keep abreast of activities of other Friends' groups or to learn more about forming a Friends of the Library, contact the Friends of the Library Committee, Public Relations Section, Library Administration Division of the American Library Association (50 E. Huron St., Chicago, IL 60611). The committee publishes a useful newsletter, *Friends of the Library—National Notebook,* and has other materials available. Groups that publish brochures, leaflets, newsletters or other items that may be of interest to Friends around the country are asked to send copies of their publications to division headquarters.

LOBBYING EFFORTS

As noted previously, most libraries are dependent on state as well as local funds for their survival. Federal programs are also crucial to local library operations. It is therefore important for librarians, Friends and library-related community groups to keep a constant dialogue flowing with state and federal legislators who affect the life of the library.

Too often, librarians feel that good things will come to those who wait. Unfortunately, the days of the benevolent legislator have disappeared along with the free lunch and the 18-cent stamp. Many librarians feel that it's acceptable for representatives of oil companies, unions or foreign nations to lobby for their interests, but libraries "are above lobbying." That belief will have to change if the library is to be heard above the din of the professional lobbyists who know what to do, who to see and when to present a point of view.

Former Congresswoman Elizabeth Holtzman made the point very clearly:

> Despite the fact that Congress couldn't function for a minute without its own library, it tends to forget how vitally important libraries are to everybody.
> You must encourage small business people in your communities to let their Representatives know how much they rely on the public libraries. Encourage teachers, lawyers, students, readers for pleasure and readers for profit, and music lovers who borrow your tapes and records, and art lovers who borrow your prints—everybody who uses your resources and depends on them, whether for recreation and entertainment or for more "serious" purposes—to let their Representatives know how important public libraries are to them.
> And tell them to speak up. Quiet voices are fine in the reading room but they won't be heard in Washington. Make your voices loud and your messages clear. Your government will have to listen. It is important to push for improved national commitment to

libraries, but there is a serious question. Can this be achieved in a budget cutting atmosphere, with proposition 13 on the ascendency?

It is crucial to make your case matter. The available information on library use is not enough. You need to improve your measuring standards. You need to exploit or bring to bear your experience with the private sector to achieve ever greater efficiency in the use of every library dollar. It is also important to speak on the state and local level—localities pay the most of libraries' budgets. This means that library quality varies based on the wealth of the particular area. Just as we recognize that school financing should move away from dependence on local tax bases, so should library financing. Efforts to bring this problem to the attention of state legislators must not be overlooked.[5]

Lobbying is not a dirty word. It is the art and practice of identifying those individuals and groups that affect the funding and operation of the library and, to put it simply, selling your cause.

Professional Associations

Reaching state and federal legislators is not as simple as attending a local council meeting. However, it can be done. Most states and many counties have established organizations that monitor state and federal legislators' views on library legislation. It is valuable to establish a formal structure for tracking library-related bills and an action plan to follow in communicating with individual legislators. There may be an occasion when pending legislation is so crucial to the library that a concentrated, community-wide campaign is necessary to influence the legislature.

If there is a strong state library association it will have a legislative committee that is active in state and county library affairs. There will be a newsletter designed to inform libraries throughout the state of various legislative programs. Often a state association will urge support or opposition to forthcoming state legislation. Local libraries will serve their interests best by heeding the advice of the legislative committee and planning an ongoing letter writing campaign to key legislators.

Obviously, most people are not going to follow the library's lead in a letter writing campaign. However, when people are alerted to the "pocket-book issue" and can be convinced that a forthcoming action by the state will either cost more in tax dollars or deny the local library funds that may have to be obtained by increasing local taxes, it is possible to arouse local sentiment to the extent that individuals will sit down and write to their legislators.

One creative, fully orchestrated statewide campaign was conducted by the West Virginia Library Commission. The commission enlisted the support of the state's 134 public libraries to raise money and generate public support for the state's libraries. Through a "Library Pin Pal" campaign, thousands of lapel pins were sold throughout the state. All pins came on cards explaining the campaign. In addition, a library "pin pal" dinner was held for the Governor and legislators as well as some 700 library supporters. Each guest received a souvenir coffee mug containing the message, "Libraries Deserve a Break, Too." Other campaigns involved selling library ties or scarves carrying the message, "Tie One on for the Library," and producing a cookbook containing a recipe for "library pie.'' The theme, "Library Pie Requires State Dough," gave state legislators the message that the first step in making "library pie" for all West Virginians was to "knead the dough."

Unfortunately, too many state organizations lack the funds to assemble a full-fledged lobbying campaign. Too often, state associations with limited treasuries must rely on the state librarian to lobby on behalf of the entire state network of public libraries.

On the national level, the American Library Association (ALA) and the American Association of School Librarians have national networks to alert state chairpersons of impending library-related legislation. A professional lobbyist representing the ALA will often propose state and local campaigns to influence congressional action on a specific bill.

Local Efforts

Local libraries can organize their own programs to monitor legislative activity. The following are a few guidelines for library administrators:

• As part of your routine reading, include copies of newsletters from state and national library groups and note data concerning bills or other legislative action that may affect the library. You also may want to assign a staff member to study specific bills before the state or national legislature. In addition, be sure to cover your own municipal government.

• Use a card file to list the names, addresses and committees of key local, state and national legislators. (This card file is also valuable for sending them the library newsletter or other publications.) Your card file should also record the date the legislator is up for reelection. Don't hesitate to write a personal letter prior to the election and ask specific questions regarding the official's position on current or forthcoming library legislation. If the official represents your district be sure to inform the community whether or not the legislator has supported the interests of the library. Although the library must not formally endorse or oppose a candidate, informing the community of a candidate's position certainly falls within the library's domain of information dissemination.

• Establish a procedure for contacting a legislator, either by letter or wire, when a specific library-related bill is due for a vote on the legislative floor. Have forms available in the library for patrons' use as well.

• Maintain an ongoing dialogue with local and system-wide libraries to assure that all receive current information regarding pending legislative action.

• Publicize—in your local newspaper, library newsletter, or Friends' newsletter—action being taken by the library to influence legislation. This action may be a mail campaign or a meeting with legislators at the state capitol. Let the community know that the library is involved. After all, if the library doesn't show that it cares about its own interests, why should anyone else?

• Invite local and state legislators to speak before library and community groups. A politician loves an audience. When he or she appears before an audience of voters concerned about the library it may pay off in support.

• Follow up your campaign to influence legislation with a personal letter to your legislator. If your library received favorable treatment, thank the legislator for his or her consideration. If your legislator opposed the interests of the library, let the individual know that you are aware of this action.

Keep in mind that by remaining on the sidelines the library stands to lose the financial support and the interest of those individuals who control the future of the library. Letter writing is an important part of your lobbying effort but certainly not the only action that you can take.

CONCLUSIONS

Successful marketing requires continuing communication between the library and those individuals who have the power to affect its operations. First and foremost among these individuals are government officials on the local, state and national level. The marketing effort begins at home. Attend public meetings and become known to your local legislators; learn the process by which tax dollars are allocated to various community groups; keep key officials informed of library activities and be alert to the needs of policy makers; remind officials that the answers to many of their questions are just a phone call away, at their local library.

Do not ignore other local leaders, including community service organizations. If there is a Friends of the Library group, work with it on a broad range of activities. If there is no group, consider starting one. The Friends are dedicated, hardworking volunteers whose aim is service to the library. A close, harmonious relationship with the Friends may be the library's best public relations asset.

Finally, remember that the library is affected by policies and events from outside the local area. Keep informed about federal and state legislative activities and communicate with legislators on an ongoing basis. Be ready to mobilize public support when a library-related bill is under consideration. Most of these bills will relate to library funding, and your lobbying efforts can be significant in convincing legislators to appropriate necessary funds for library operations.

Fund raising is, of course, among the primary reasons for marketing the library. Some hints on raising money from the private sector appear in the next chapter.

FOOTNOTES

1. Harold L. Roth, "Public Relations for a Developing Library or Starting from Scratch," in *Public Relations for Libraries,* ed. Allan Angoff (Westport, CT: Greenwood Press, 1973), p. 226-27.

2. Sarah Leslie Wallace, *Friends of the Library* (Chicago, IL: American Library Association, 1962), p. 32.

3. M.G. de Chazeau, "The Cornell Public Library and its Friends," *Wilson Library Bulletin* 31 (March 1957): 517-20.

4. Wallace, op. cit., p. 67.

5. Elizabeth Holtzman, "Libraries and the Federal Scene," *Bookmark* (Fall 1979): 264.

5

Fund Raising

Libraries today are increasingly reliant on fundraising campaigns to augment the support they receive from tax dollars. Although a full-scale campaign to raise money for a new building or other major project occurs perhaps once or twice in a library's history, there is a constant need to supplement the library's income for everyday operations. Sources for these additional funds range from small local contributions to government and foundation grants.

Fund raising is an art that often requires professional expertise. For example, studies have shown that simply varying the salutation of a letter can increase response to a direct mail campaign. Professional direct mail designers will perform test upon test before selecting a particular method of approaching an audience. On the other hand, librarians know their own institutions best and are often better able to communicate the library's needs. And, of course, many libraries cannot afford the services of professional fundraising organizations. Even if professional help is engaged, it is vital for the library director and staff to be fully involved in the planning and implementation of any fundraising activities.

Whether soliciting money for a political candidate, a library or a subscription to the *Reader's Digest,* the basics are the same. A product, idea or, in the case of the library, a *need,* must be sold to the public.

The methods used for library fund raising will, of course, vary with specific need as well as with the characteristics and financial resources of the community. A high-powered, direct mail campaign aimed at the total population of a large city may be a wasted effort, since only a small segment of the community is likely to have the resources and desire to support the library. Unfortunately, the library may lack the resources to identify that segment, i.e., to make the basic determination: who should be solicited?

PLANNING A BUILDING OR EXPANSION CAMPAIGN

Probably the largest fundraising effort undertaken by a public library is for the construction of a new building or the expansion of the existing structure. Such a project must be approached with great care. Says Harold L. Roth:

> It is important to avoid building development before analyzing the needs to be served. (Buildings stand out as great contributions in a political campaign.) Even if an architect has been selected, he has to be kept at bay. The library administration has to be able to study the situation and come up with proposed solutions in every possible arena of action. The director has to be specific about some plans and vague about others. He does, however, have to push in a forward direction to show progress, but delay the building until cooperative forces can be assayed. All this must be accomplished within a restricted budget that has to be shared with other agencies under a master budget code umbrella.[1]

Cost Estimates

In assessing the building needs of the library, it is the responsibility of the Board of Trustees to initiate the action. Too often the financial requirements of a new building or expansion are underestimated for fear that too high a price tag will scare away contributors. The result of "low-balling" an estimate will be disastrous.

Once the basic decision is made to embark on a building program, the library Board should consult a reputable architect. In most cases, the Board has already made preliminary inquiries into costs by asking a local architect for rough estimates. Too often, these initial "ball park" numbers expand into "stadium" figures. Since any valid cost estimate requires considerable investment of the architect's time to analyze the needs of the library and the many facets of construction, an architect may require a fee for developing the initial set of numbers for the Board. Thus, money may well have to be spent even before a firm decision is made to undertake an expansion program. If a community is fortunate enough to have a local architect volunteer his or her services in providing the initial cost figures, so much the better. However, before accepting the gift of a free architectural consultation, be sure there are absolutely no commitments made to the contributor. Although most communities require formal, sealed bids on any large municipal construction projects, bad feelings can easily be generated by a misunderstanding at this stage.

A common failing in trying to determine complete cost estimates is overlooking the ongoing maintenance expenditures following construction. Even a relatively small library addition will affect future budgets. Energy costs will increase, additional staff may be required, and repair and housekeeping costs will be incurred. These increased expenditures can rarely be absorbed in a public solicitation of funds.

One small suburban library was understandably eager to accept the generous gift of a building addition, designed to be used solely as a program room. Unfortunately, no consideration was given to staff requirements, energy needs or who would implement the various programming activities for which the room was intended. As could have been predicted, energy costs increased by more than 10% the first year the new room was in operation (and this increase was prior to the unexpected, dramatic OPEC oil price hikes). Programming the first year was practically nil. Although the room was meant for presentation of musical events, no one considered the fact that the library didn't own a piano and certainly lacked the funds to acquire one.

It was only through the work of the local Friends of the Library that the room was put to use. The Friends acquired a piano and provided a grant to the library to hire a part-time program director. At the end of the grant period, the program director's salary was absorbed·into the library's budget along with several other costs that had never been considered: piano tuning, slide and motion picture projector, improved fire detection system, telephone and carpet cleaning. Fortunately, most of the library's annual expenditures for the new room are recouped through rental fees. Custodial service, for example, is paid in full by any group that desires to use the room. Yet, many library additions add an unexpected burden to the budget without the possibility of receiving reimbursement through use fees.

Bond Issues

Before embarking upon a full-fledged money raising campaign, the library should consider several possible steps. The first, and perhaps the most important, is to resolve the question of a possible bond issue. Interest rates, even for municipalities with a solid credit rating, are at an all-time high, and it is entirely possible that the cost of borrowing money will increase still further. A long-term bond will have to be guaranteed by the issuing government body and is a long-term financial encumbrance on the community. Generally, based on mid-1981 interest rates of about 12% (for tax free bonds), a 20-year bond will require a payback of roughly 3½ times the amount of the original dollar total of the bond. Thus, a $500,000 bond will cost the taxpayers of the community more than $1.5 million over the 20-year period. However, for the community that has little or no chance of raising the amount of capital through gifts or grants, a bond issue may be the only way to go if the library is to be expanded.

A bond issue presents a further complication, however. Most communities require all bond issues to be voted upon at a public referendum. Thus, the library is placed in an arena it doesn't want to be in: politics. The library, however, cannot afford to take a back seat and claim to be "above politics." By so doing, there is a strong chance that a proposed bond will be defeated and the library expansion with it.

This doesn't mean that partisanship must enter the picture. As a matter of fact, once the library bond issue becomes a partisan question, not only does the bond issue itself face a good chance of defeat, but the library becomes identified as a political institution. In the past, many library bond issues have been defeated. The majority of these defeats have had no relation to the issue of community improvement. Voters rarely have an opportunity to communicate feelings on expenditures directly to a government. It's much easier to simply vote "no," regardless of the issue. Thus, a major selling campaign is required if the library is to convince voters that a "yes" vote on a bond issue will mean a better library, an improved community and, in some cases, higher property values.

The library should enlist the advice and support of the local League of Women Voters during this politically sensitive period. Other nonpartisan groups should be contacted and asked for formal support. These groups, including civic clubs, fraternal organizations, labor unions and neighborhood associations, may be able to influence public opinion toward passage of the bond issue and to get out the vote on election day.

The Campaign Committee

Whether or not a bond issue is involved, when the library Board has made a commitment to proceed with a broad community fundraising campaign, the Board should establish a campaign committee to assist in all phases of planning and implementation. Since the committee should represent a wide range of community interests, it should include key members of the government and labor structure, corporate representatives, educators, foundation and religious leaders and civic leaders.

There is always the desire to try to identify a few wealthy members of the community and use membership on the committee as a bridge to a generous donation. There is an obvious potential problem in adopting this strategy. Not only is there no guarantee that the "fat cat" invited to be a member of the committee will indeed make a contribution, but selecting one or two individuals to join an "exclusive" community committee is likely to offend other possible donors. There is no easy solution to the question of who is to serve on the committee. However, as the group is being determined by the Board, discretion should be the watchword.

GETTING THE CAMPAIGN UNDERWAY

With a firm estimate of the amount of money required and the establishment of a fundraising committee, the next step is the planning and development of the fundraising strategy. In almost all cases, seed money is required to operate a major campaign. Brochures and posters must be printed, mailings must be made, ads in local newspapers should be considered and a continuing publicity program must be designed. The amount of money required to operate a full campaign will, of course, depend on the size of the campaign, numbers of people to be contacted by direct mail, frequency of mailings and amount of paid advertising, if any. These data must all be considered well before the campaign gets underway.

Establishing a kick off date for the campaign is a must. Along with this date, campaign planners should actually program a calendar with the dates for each mailing, community meetings, library events related to the campaign, newspaper ad program, spot announcements on the local radio, TV or cable stations, etc. Preparation for printing and mailing should be based on these dates, as should dates for the flood of press releases and announcements that should flow from the library's campaign offices.

The campaign committee must also plan a close working relationship with local civic, professional and business organizations. Not only will many of these groups represent prime donors, but their ongoing cooperation is essential. Following the initial announcement of construction plans, the library should program events that involve local groups. The library is emphasizing again the service it provides all aspects of the community. After each program, the campaign committee uses the opportunity to illustrate the need for the library's expansion and to make community leaders aware that money is needed to run the campaign as well as for the actual construction.

During these early stages, the help of local business leaders may be enlisted. Stickers for store windows, or plaques, are presented to donors. Buttons with clever sayings can be sold in local stores, as well as in the library or by mail. As previously mentioned, the West Virginia Library Commission designed special pins stating: "Be A Library Pin Pal." Pins or special labels, plaques, buttons, banners, etc. are available from numerous suppliers of premium goods. (Check your local *Yellow Pages* under "Premium Goods" and "Flags & Banners.")

THE PUBLIC CAMPAIGN

With an established budget for the campaign and a group of boosters behind the campaign, you are ready to embark on the next phase: a full public solicitation.

Mailings

Community-wide mailings must be considered, but care should be exercised. As previously noted, the size and demographics of the community will often determine the extent of the mail campaign. A large library with many branches will not solicit donations from all city residents, but only from those near the planned library expansion. Smaller communities will often mail to all residents plus neighboring communities that use the library frequently. There is no hard and fast rule to determine the size or scope of a direct mail campaign. And there is no rule that establishes a ratio between brochures mailed and dollars received.

Lists for mailings must represent the most current names and addresses possible. In most cases, the city or town clerk will be able to supply names of those currently on the tax roles. These are the lists used by the municipality to mail out tax statements. Unfortunately, since most tax lists are based on real estate holdings, apartment dwellers are usually omitted. In areas heavily populated by apartment dwellers, it is possible to obtain lists of apartment addresses from professional list brokers. List brokers are also able to provide lists by individual zip codes or, in many cases, actual street names. Rarely, however, will a list broker be able to include the names of current residents with the street name list. However, for little or no additional cost, the broker is able to insert a slug before the street address. The slug can read: Occupant, Resident, Current Resident, etc. Special slugs such as Library Patron, Library Friend, etc., can also be inserted.

The price of lists available from professional brokers varies. As an average, however, estimate paying between $40 and $50 per thousand names. Labels prepared in a special format (e.g., gummed, self-adhesive labels) will add to the cost per thousand.

Brochures

The design and printing of brochures is another cost that cannot be ignored in any major fundraising campaign. A professional looking brochure is important. Although a press release or newsletter can be printed on a mimeograph machine, asking the community to donate a significant sum of money requires a more elaborate publication. A four-color brochure is an extremely attractive way to sell your message, but in most cases the cost of four-color printing will be too high. A crisp, well-designed, one- or two-color mailing piece can be just as effective.

The key is selling your message. The brochure must accomplish two tasks: inform readers that the library is an essential element in the community, and convince them that the new addition or building is essential. How will the community benefit by donating? How will the library be enhanced by the expenditure? And, conversely, would the community be hurt if the requested funds are not raised?

Where possible, architectural plans or renderings should be included in the brochure. The public should be able to visualize how the forthcoming expansion will blend with the current building or the library's surroundings. Facts and figures are important. How many new volumes will the new expansion allow? How much more parking space will there be? What new facilities will be added?

Although the total cost of the structure can't be glossed over, there are ways to make even the largest expenditure more palatable. For example, in a community with a population of 100,000, a $500,000 library expansion means but $5 a person. The cost of a motion picture today is about $5 a person. The brochure might ask a family to "forgo a trip to the movies for a major library expansion that will last forever." A community bond issue brings the cost per person or family even lower. Since the bond is paid off over a period of many years, the annual per capita tax burden is usually measured in pennies.

Displays and Handouts

An active campaign in the library itself must also be prepared. Posters, flyers and detailed descriptions of the desired expansion plans should be on view. If there is an architect's model of the new building or planned expansion, be sure that it is highly visible in the library. Special bookmarks, printed with an appeal to support the fund campaign, can be inserted in all books checked out. A running total of money collected can be reported on various graphic displays. The thermometer device is a familiar display used by many communities. Press releases giving the weekly total keep attention focused on the campaign.

LARGE CONTRIBUTIONS AND GRANTS

An alternative or adjunct to a community-wide fundraising venture is an appeal to individuals or organizations with the resources to make substantial donations. Although it is rare that a single individual, foundation or corporation will fund an entire library addition or new structure, the potential should not be ignored. More likely, an individual or organization may be inclined to give a major contribution to start off the fund campaign. When a library plans to build several new rooms, it is possible to "sell" a room to one of the more affluent members of the community: that is, the room will be named after the individual or a relative the individual wishes to honor, in return for a gift enabling its construction.

Appealing to the community spirit of large companies in the area is also a worthwhile effort. Contact should be made directly with the company's chief operating officer, first by formal letter and then, if possible, by a personal meeting.

It is also possible to solicit funds outside the local community by applying for a government, foundation or corporate grant. Unfortunately, the overwhelming majority of such applications (an estimated 75%-80%) are turned down.[2] Nonetheless, private foundations alone contributed more than $36.5 million to libraries in 1979. By far the largest segment of this amount ($20.5 million) went to academic libraries; approximately $2.4 million was allocated to public libraries.[3]

A good source of information on grants is The Foundation Center, with headquarters in New York City and field offices in San Francisco, Washington and Cleveland, plus cooperating collections in 50 states, Mexico, Puerto Rico and the Virgin Islands. The Foundation Center offers inexpensive seminars on grantsmanship throughout the United States and has an extensive library of relevant materials, in addition to publishing its own books and periodicals. Another organization is the Grantsmanship Center in Los Angeles, which also runs seminars and publishes a newsletter six times a year.

The *Bowker Annual of Library & Book Trade Information* and the *Annual Register of Grant Support* (Chicago: Marquis Who's Who, Inc.) are standard reference works that provide valuable information to libraries interested in seeking grant aid. *Funding Alternatives for Libraries* (Chicago: American Library Association, 1979), edited by Patricia Senn Breivik and E. Burr Gibson, is a collection of essays on various aspects of fund raising, including program planning, lobbying and government and foundation funding. Another guide is *Grant Money & How To Get It: A Handbook for Librarians,* by Richard W. Boss, which lists private foundations, as well as federal sources and state foundation directories. This book offers many helpful hints on how to contact potential funding sources, how to develop a proposal and how to follow up on a proposal.

Boss emphasizes the importance of appointing a grants coordinator to learn grantsmanship techniques, identify sources of funds, establish contacts with potential funding organizations and oversee proposals from the planning stage onward. He is convinced that a librarian is better equipped for the job than a professional fund raiser:

> A part-time grants coordinator is preferable to retaining a professional fund raiser. A fund raiser takes a proposal idea prepared by the library and develops it into a formal grant proposal. The proposal will usually be well organized and attractive in appearance, but it will often lack real substance because the writer is generally not a professional librarian. This fact may come through to the funding source in preliminary review, and the library runs the real risk of not being able to respond adequately in negotiations that follow selection by the funding source. The library may also be ill prepared to perform after a grant is awarded. The money expended for such services is better invested in the training of a grants coordinator for the library. If the library cannot do so, an alternative would be a joint venture with one or more other libraries.[4]

Grant money is available for purposes other than construction of library facilities. The

Council on Library Resources awards grants for research, development and demonstration projects related to library operations, mainly in academic and research libraries. Other public and private agencies give money for acquisitions, continuing education for librarians, special services to the handicapped and other programs.

ONGOING FUND RAISING

Although the major fundraising effort is a rarity, periodic fund raising should be part of the library's ongoing effort. The purchase of a new microfilm reader-printer, installation of a security system, an addition to a special collection or replacement of a heating system are the kinds of expenses that often strain or exceed the normal operating budget. A library should have a plan for such periodic fundraising programs. Often they are run by the Friends of the Library. Some Friends' groups prefer to avoid expenditures for capital equipment, using monies received to improve book and periodical collections. Others are active fund raisers for any special needs, including construction, that may not be covered in the regular operating budget.

The library should constantly maintain a "want list" of such items. These special items may range in cost from a few hundred dollars to several thousand dollars. Then, if an individual or group asks what specific items are needed by the library, the director has a list available and can sit down with the potential donor and discuss intelligently the ways and means of giving a gift.

In addition to a list of desired items, the library should maintain an ongoing file of previous and potential donors. Besides names and addresses, this record should list the amount of last donation, date and any special areas of gift giving. Although many donors want their gifts to be limited strictly to books or periodicals, others may be more interested in the library building or grounds. A donor who specifies that a contribution is to be used for a particular purpose—for example, the acquisition of materials related to gardening— must have that request honored. Such restrictions should be indicated on the file card.

Endowment Funds

Some donors may wish to establish a permanent fund, for instance, as a memorial to a parent. In most cases, an individual donor will make the initial contact with the library. However, it is important for the community to be aware that the library is in need of such bequests. The library director should encourage a potential donor to discuss his or her wishes with an attorney before making a commitment. There may be important tax advantages as well as possible disadvantages in establishing an individual endowment fund. The library itself should seek legal advice on the proper form of receiving bequests and investing gift funds. The library, as a public institution, is governed by state and federal law regarding the types of investments that can be made with endowment funds.

A check given to the library with no strings attached is not a restricted gift. Thus, the trustees must use their best judgment as to how the money will be used. However, when a donor establishes a formal bequest, either by will or other legal instrument, the trustees may be required to act in a fiduciary capacity. For example, an individual who establishes a formal trust may name the library Board as either sole trustee of the specific trust or co-trustee with a local bank. Management of the funds then becomes a legal responsibility of the library Board. Again, proper legal counsel will best answer questions on both the management of the endowment and the expenditure of income generated.

Endowment funds can be used to establish and maintain entire memorial libraries, building wings, special rooms and collections. Such a gift can also be used to provide a continuing memorial series of lectures, films, exhibits or other programs.

Obviously, the gift of a room or major collection involves a considerable sum of money. For individuals interested in making a far more modest bequest, consider an endowment fund used to acquire a few special books a year. For example, a gift of $1000 established as an endowment can earn about $150 a year at mid-1981 money market fund interest rates. This amount can purchase about a dozen general trade books or several more expensive art books. Special book plates stating that a particular book was acquired with money from the XYZ Memorial Fund should be printed and affixed inside the front cover of all books purchased with income from the special fund. If possible, records should be maintained stating which specific books in the collection were acquired with these funds. An annual personal letter from the director or trustee to the funds' donors should state how fund money was spent. These letters serve as reminders that the fund is indeed active and may also encourage additional cash gifts.

Publicizing Donations

The establishment of a special fund is an occasion to send a press release to the local paper and radio or TV station. A picture of a donor presenting the library director with a check serves to promote additional fund giving, as well as a record of formal acceptance and thanks. However, just as many donors expect to see their names and photographs in the local paper (in fact failure to publicize gifts may seriously offend a donor), there are individuals who wish to remain anonymous. Naturally, this request must be honored. Failure to honor an individual's request to remain anonymous can not only prove embarrassing to the individual but may seriously hamper the library's future fundraising campaign.

The library should prepare a brochure stating the library's interest in and policy towards receiving gift funds. List some of the recent offerings and state how the library has spent special bequests. If there is an ongoing want list of specific items, the brochure can be used to spread the word. Be careful, however, in estimating the cost of items on your want list. The brochure may be in existence for several years and you can count on the cost of most library-related items to increase.

Remember that many items the library may need will also require additional funds to maintain. If the donor does not include these additional expenditures in the bequest, the library will have to plan other ways of raising the funds. And the library must include these maintenance costs in the planning of its own want list.

PROFESSIONAL FUND RAISERS

Periodic fundraising campaigns should involve the entire library staff, Friends and as many members of the community as possible. There are also outside groups available to work with organizations in raising money. These professional fundraising groups can be located in most *Yellow Pages* under "Fund Raising Counselors & Organizations." The groups listed specialize in assisting charitable organizations to plan and operate their funding programs. Some groups have had more experience with public libraries, other groups with academic libraries.

The professional fund raiser is certainly not for every library. It is usually the large public or academic libraries that can best use the expertise and sophisticated campaigning methods available through fundraising organizations. For one thing, there is a cost involved. Although the cost or fee is a negotiable item, most professional fundraising firms charge a flat, predetermined sum for the services provided. Some organizations, such as American Fund Raising Services (Boston and New York), provide a total multi-year campaign including reports on list effectiveness, area penetration, income penetration, etc. The cost to a library can only be found by shopping around and comparing the services offered by several professional organizations.

Large libraries may find it cost-effective to use an outside agency for fund raising and for a total marketing effort. For example, the New York Public Library hired the advertising firm of Muir Cornelius Moore Inc. to produce a complete package; new stationery and a new library logo were designed. The agency consulted with the library in preparing the direct mail campaigns and coined the library's slogan, "The Lions are hungry!" referring to the famous stone figures at the entrance to the main building. (See Figure 5.1.)

The use of a public relations firm and the selection of a specific firm are complicated issues. According to Joyce Yaeger, Director of Public Relations, New York Public Library, "There are so many aspects to a library. It is not as simple as selling a product. An outside group can be most helpful for specific projects or to use as a consulting group when the skills and talents are lacking within a library. Unfortunately, it is extremely difficult to find a public relations firm that understands the complexities of a library."[5] This thought echoes Boss's view on grants coordinators: librarians understand their institutions' needs and can communicate them best.

THE MEMBERSHIP CONCEPT

Many libraries use the membership concept to raise funds. The New York Public Library, for example, bases its fundraising program on generating a large membership list. Its campaign is not periodic or cyclical but is a full-time, year-round effort. Approximately 2 million letters are mailed annually to individuals, corporations and foundations within a 50-mile radius of the city. Recently, the library mailed solicitation letters to former New York City residents who had moved to Florida. This campaign was highly successful.

In 1981, New York Public had built its membership list to include more than 19,000

Figure 5.1   Direct Mail Piece Prepared for the New York Public Library's Fundraising Campaign

the Lions are Hungry!

Dear Reader:

Two famous lions on Manhattan's Fifth Avenue are hungry. And that's too bad, because keeping them fed is important to people like you and me--people who care about our rich heritage and preserving it for those who will come after us.

The lions I'm talking about are Patience and Fortitude, gentle guardians of the world's busiest library. It is, of course, The New York Public Library, one of a handful of great research libraries and a true national asset. Located at the heart of New York City, The New York Public Library offers nothing less than a complete record of human achievement in almost every field of endeavor, in almost every language. It is a treasure trove open to any adult, accessible by visit, telephone or letter.

Any picture you might have of a library as a quiet, sparsely inhabited place disappears the minute you set foot in this Library. Business researchers, scholars, students and average citizens from all over the world pour in and out of The New York Public Library's doors, making it one of the most active and essential places in this great city.

By feeding the lions now you will help us keep those doors open.

Perhaps you have always assumed that The New York Public Library was tax-supported. Our neighborhood branches in Manhattan, The Bronx and Staten Island are, but the world-famous Research Library depends on private gifts for almost two-thirds of its support. The Research Library collections are housed in the Central Building on Fifth Avenue, its Annex on the West Side, the library at Lincoln Center and the Schomburg Center in Harlem.

The other third comes from annual government grants, which are not automatic and must be applied for each year. Because our Research Library is recognized as a national institution, one of the larg- est of those grants comes from the National Endowment for the

The New York Public Library

Fifth Avenue at 42nd Street ● New York, New York 10018 ● (212) 930-0662

Astor, Lenox and Tilden Foundations

Friends who donated $25 or more, 13,000 who donated less than $25, 1000 corporations, and 800 foundations. The anticipated 1981 income from this effort is between $8 and $9 million, at a cost of about $1 million.

One interesting aspect of the New York Public's campaign experience occurred when the library decided to abandon its use of premiums. When various premiums were used to encourage membership, the library had the common problem of inventory, delivery, etc. When it was decided to drop the use of premiums it was expected that both new memberships and renewals might be discouraged. The library found to the contrary: membership did not suffer at all. In fact, the percentage of those who responded to mail appeals actually increased slightly.

LIBRARY PROGRAMS AND SALES

Libraries can program various events that raise money while they provide real community service. Consider, for example, presenting plays, concerts, lectures or films for a modest admission fee. (See Chapter 3 for a discussion of special programs and fees.)

Also, consider off-beat ideas. One library recently arranged for a representative from a New York City auction house to spend the day in the community evaluating and identifying personal items of potential historic or monetary value. Silver, furniture, paintings and drawings, china and glass were all culled from people's attics for "Heirloom Day." The fee to have an item evaluated was $7. There was no limit to the number of items an individual or family could bring before the experts. Although the auction house received a fee, there was more than enough left over to produce income for the library.

Other ideas include selling fresh oranges, grapefruit or other fruit, purchased in bulk at a discounted rate from one of the many groves in Florida or Texas. Macadamia nuts from Hawaii or pecans from the South may be the basis of a regional theme for a fund-raising campaign. A few words of caution. Although there are many types of food or other specialty items that the library can sell (check a premium catalog for a list of items and locations of dealers) the library doesn't want to get into the food or merchandise business. Whenever possible, try to presell items before taking receipt of inventory. With food items, it is essential to write an order and accept payment before delivery. There is nothing worse than a few dozen bushels of ripe fruit rotting in the library.

Renting Library Space

The library fortunate enough to have a program or meeting room can always raise revenue by renting the room to other groups within the community. To do this requires a firm policy established by the Board of Trustees. Several basic questions must be addressed: Can the room be rented by groups who in turn wish to use the library facilities to raise income for their own behalf? Can the room be rented by a group for use solely by its own membership—that is, can certain segments of the community be turned away at the door? Can food or drink be served? What about smoking regulations? Will there be different room rental rates for local civic groups as opposed to groups from outside the community? Are any community groups entitled to free use of the room? Will the rates be different for use at night, Sunday or periods when the library is not open?

These questions must all be discussed by the Board before developing a firm room-rental policy. (It should be remembered that the library, as a public institution, should do all it can to bring the public to the library even if there is no direct financial benefit. Since the library becomes the center of community attention and interest, its own marketing effort will be enhanced.)

Selling Used Books

Perhaps one of the more common methods of raising income is from the sale of de-accessioned materials. When a library weeds its shelves there is often the question of what to do with 10 copies of last year's best-sellers. Often these books can be donated to a local hospital, school or veterans' home. Some libraries use discards as the basis of an annual book sale (see Chapter 3). Other libraries maintain a shelf or single location within the library where used books are sold. The price of used books can vary, but usually it simplifies bookkeeping and the problem of determining a book's worth to simply place a single price on any hardcover and another price on any softcover book. Reference books or special items may be priced higher.

Books that have outlived their usefulness in the library don't necessarily have to be sold at the library. Many community bookstores arrange to sell library books at a substantial discount, reimbursing the library for books sold. In Ardmore, PA, for example, the local bookstore provides a section where "hurt books" are sold at discount. All "hurt books" are former library discards. The local library, of course, benefits from the sale without having to concern itself with inventory control, possible sales taxes or managing the selling of merchandise.

Hidden Treasures

Periodically, the library should also inventory its collection to determine if a hidden gem has found its way into the stacks. Usually, a library will need the services of a professional antiquarian or rare book expert. The Scarsdale (NY) Public Library recently hired author and library-consultant Lee Ash to evaluate its collection. Although the primary purpose of the evaluation was to determine strengths and weaknesses in the various subject areas, a few surprises did result. An early 20th century reference set on fruit growing in New York State (published by the N.Y. State Department of Agriculture) contained beautiful four-color illustrations and, according to Ash, was quite valuable. Although the work had been in the reference collection for decades, no librarian could recall ever having used the material. The 10-volume set was sold through a rare book dealer and brought the library money from a source it least expected.

Many librarians are now well aware of the value of some of the illustrations contained in early periodicals. For example, *Harper's Weekly* and *Leslie's Illustrated* published many of the first woodcut engravings of American artists Winslow Homer and Frederic Remington, as well as the political cartoons of Thomas Nast. Many of these drawings, originally printed and sold for pennies, are now very valuable. The librarian who has duplicated the text of these early periodicals on microform and plans to discard the hard copies should consider the potential value first. Also, many early periodicals with no particular intellectual or artistic value are interesting to collectors of historical mementos. Early issues of *Time, Life, The Saturday Evening Post, Look* and *Fortune* can be sold to dealers for prices ranging from a few dollars an issue to more than $25 an issue. Complete collections of *National Geographic, American Heritage,* etc., can also be sold to collectors. Many of these hidden treasures are buried in the recesses of the library simply awaiting discovery.

CONCLUSION

As public funds tighten, more and more libraries find it necessary to mount aggressive fundraising campaigns. It is important that these efforts be carefully planned and that they involve the library director and staff, even when professional fund raisers are hired. Campaigns to fund major projects, such as the construction of a new building or addition, often require a bond issue. Wealthy individuals, foundations and corporations may also be approached for substantial donations. Community-wide mailings should be undertaken with caution. The support of community leaders and a steady publicity effort are essential to the success of any fundraising campaign.

Libraries must plan ongoing fundraising activities, as well as one-time-only campaigns. Maintaining a want list of desired items and a file of previous donors is useful. Endowment funds, both large and small, should be sought by the library director. Other fundraising methods include the membership concept, the sale of used books and other products, renting the library's program room, charging admission to special events and selling valuable but little-used items from the library's collection.

This chapter and the preceding ones have concentrated on the needs and marketing techniques of public libraries. Chapter 6 will offer some guidelines for nonpublic libraries, particularly in academic and corporate settings.

FOOTNOTES

1. Harold L. Roth, "Public Relations for a Developing Library or Starting from Scratch," in *Public Relations for Libraries,* ed. Allan Angoff (Westport, CT: Greenwood Press, 1973), p. 225.

2. Richard W. Boss, *Grant Money & How To Get It: A Handbook for Librarians* (New York: R.R. Bowker Co., 1980), p. 1.

3. *Bowker Annual of Library & Book Trade Information* (New York: R.R. Bowker Co., 1980), p. 278.

4. Boss, op. cit., p. 23.

5. Telephone conversation with author.

6

Marketing Academic and Special Libraries

Academic libraries and the host of libraries serving the needs of business, government, research organizations and other special-interest groups have many of the same marketing needs and problems as the public library. The need for funding is ever present, as is the need to educate the "community" (e.g., students and faculty, managers, researchers) that the library is its vital information center.

Although many of the same problems exist in both public and nonpublic libraries, there are elements unique to the nonpublic library. The constant threat of loss of tax revenue from a municipal government is absent. (Government libraries and public colleges, however, are concerned about financial aid from government coffers.) The potential problem of community pressure groups is usually lacking. Although the academic library will undoubtedly feel pressure from various school departments to enhance a special collection or subject area, in many cases these pressures are not only manageable but should be encouraged. Faculty are likely to better appreciate the importance of the library if they work with librarians to develop acquisitions policies that meet the needs of their departments.

Nonpublic libraries have their own financial pressures. While academic libraries do not have to prove the necessity for their existence (one could hardly run an educational institution without a library), they do have to compete with other educational resources for steadily eroding funds. Special libraries, or information centers, in profit-making organizations must compete with other departments for the company dollar. And the costs of operating a library or information center are rising rapidly, particularly in institutions that offer sophisticated computer services.

Thus nonpublic libraries must pay attention to marketing. They must increase their level of service to their institutions and must ensure that their parent organizations recognize their value and respond to their needs. In an academic setting, this means communicating with faculty, administration, governing boards and alumni, as well as students. In other special libraries, it means gaining the ear of top management, as well as researchers and other personnel who make more direct use of library services.

BASICS OF ACADEMIC LIBRARY PROMOTION

The academic library should develop the same type of public information program as the public library. However, since the academic library's "patron" can be more clearly defined, the question "Who should I tell my story to?" becomes much simpler. For example, it is obvious that the school administration—the group that pays the bills—must know whenever the library prepares an important new exhibit or display, publishes a major bibliography, acquires special equipment or receives a bequest. Similarly, the faculty (often drawn to a school or university because of the resources of the library) must be kept informed. George S. Bobinski, of the School of Library Science, University of Kentucky, suggests that "Academic librarians could well use the mail to welcome incoming new faculty—even before they arrive on campus. They could be provided information about the library and asked for reading lists and other library needs months in advance of their arrival on campus."[1]

The largest patron group, of course, is made up of students, and the best way to communicate with them is through the school newspaper. A periodic column written by a library staff member or public information specialist can be very effective. A meeting between the library director and the editor of the school paper may lead to the assignment of a student reporter to cover library affairs. Having a reporter include the library as part of his or her beat will help to spread news of library activities still further.

The campus radio and television station are other outlets that should be investigated by the aggressive library public information specialist. Book reviews, author interviews, literary discussions or debates involving students and faculty, new book announcements, etc., are all items that lend themselves to an audio or visual format.

The library director should assign a staff member the responsibility of working with the various campus media outlets. The individual must be knowledgeable about student and faculty interests and problems, as well as about library operations. Often the choice of a student aid (perhaps one majoring in communications) can work in the library's best interest.

Reaching Faculty Members

With the continued development of new technologies, it is increasingly important for the academic librarian to develop marketing programs directed toward faculty members. For example, many scholars, used to old-fashioned research techniques, are totally unaware that their own library has a computer-based information retrieval service that can create a tailored bibliography in hours instead of months. Some schools have adopted the position that library skills are as important an element in a student's total education as any major course of study. Although this trend is not catching the imagination of many educators, a good library-faculty liaison can encourage integration of library skills as an instructional element.

Developing a formal program to establish a liaison between the library and academic departments has been tried successfully at several institutions. Dr. Laurence Miller, who established a liaison program while director of the University Library, East Texas State University, defines liaison work as:

> . . . a formal, structured activity in which professional library staff systematically meet with teaching faculty to discuss stratagems for directly supporting their instructional needs and those of the students. Such individual conferences can be general in purpose or have a specific objective such as orientation to a new service. Liaison work can be a part-time or full-time activity. In either case it differs fundamentally from the patterns of occasional contacts that have always been made and sometimes initiated by librarians.[2]

Developing a liaison program does require a library staff with able personnel and, perhaps more importantly, personnel interested in the program. The staff must have the time to devote to the function. Since in many cases time can be equated with money, some libraries are unable to devote as much effort to such a program as they would like.

The librarian serving as a liaison must do more than use the opportunity to "sell" the latest in library services. It is just as important to listen to comments, complaints, requests and general suggestions that may lead to improved library service. Once these suggestions have been voiced, it is equally important for the liaison person to report them to the appropriate person within the library. To be told by the chairperson of the psychology department that increased acquisitions of psychology periodicals should be a top priority, and to let that request be ignored, will result in counterproductive public relations. The request should be passed on to the serials librarian for evaluation. A letter or memo from the serials librarian to the chairperson of the psychology department, acknowledging receipt of the request, would serve to improve the library's image. Even if all requests cannot be honored (and it's safe to assume that they cannot), an explanation as to why a certain request cannot be granted and an invitation from the librarian to keep the dialogue flowing will show the library's interest in maintaining communications.

To assure a smooth liaison effort, it is also most important that the library's internal communications are open. The liaison librarians must be kept informed of activities occurring in all parts of the library. According to Miller,

> Liaison work is one of the few potential effective methods we have to make an impact on the problem of the nonuser. At the same time, it can assist in maintaining the library's viability as the primary campus information agency. It is, however, a method that is vulnerable and one that requires continuous follow-up, excellent internal communications between those who are involved and those who are not, sustained interest, and a willingness to share and learn from experience within a given academic setting.[3]

David Taylor, director of the Robert B. House Undergraduate Library, University of North Carolina, Chapel Hill, has taken the concept of keeping the faculty informed a step further. During the school year the library publishes a monthly newsletter directed to the faculty. (See Figure 6.1.) Articles are devoted to two broad library-related areas: specific information about the school library and general information about national library trends,

Figure 6.1   University of North Carolina Library — Faculty Newsletter

University of North Carolina
Library

Chapel Hill   27514
     ISSN: 0468-5725

June, 1981   No. 406

The Information Explosion and the Library

The Least Publishable Unit

The Least Publishable Unit (LPU) is a phenomenon only recently encountered in scholarly literature, especially in medicine and biology. LPU is a name given to a tendency of authors to fragment a piece of research into the maximum number of articles. These may be a short article on a project with preliminary results followed soon by a final report. Or a study of several variables relating to a disease may be separated into three or four papers and published in different journals.

The cause of the LPU appears to be the "Publish or Perish" syndrome. The more published articles that can be gotten out of a research project, the better for the author. But not the better for the library and the indexer and the reader.

As William J. Broad explains in the March 13 issue of Science, "This fragmentation contributes to a host of problems, not the least being the sheer growth of the literature. One estimate holds that Index Medicus for 1985 will weigh more than 1 ton." (Science vol. 211, 13 March 1981, p. 1137) It certainly makes the work of the researcher more difficult when he must run down several references only to find that many duplicate the data of others. It makes the job of the teacher and the student more difficult when several articles with only shades of different information must be read and digested to understand a mechanism that might have been documented in one well-rounded article.

Robert W. Buddemeier and Jesse Roth, writing in the May first issue of Science, point out other factors causing the LPU. Some funding agencies dictate time tables for research projects, including publication of results. As journals and fields proliferate, authors who want diverse specialists to read their research must publish in different journals catering to those specialties. The journal editors themselves may contribute to the LPU because of their rigid im-

positions of space limitations. (Science vol 212, 1 May 1981, p. 494)

Suggestions for curing the LPU do not sound encouraging. Careful reviewing could abort an article that is only slightly different from one already published, but how can every reviewer know all the literature that intimately or be aware of manuscripts accepted but not yet published by another journal? Reviewers could also be sensitive enough to see that a paper was not a complete report of a research project and send it back to the author, but that is even less likely to be one hundred percent effective. Committees reviewing credentials could also take

developments, new technology and information that could affect the faculty. During the summer, the library publishes a single issue, usually devoted to a single topic or theme, e.g., "Services to Support Teaching."

Reaching the Students

A library can devise many special programs to make students more aware of library services and needs. Sometimes a program can involve a large portion of the student body. For example, George Bobinski writes of a college library director who persuaded student leaders to help the library raise funds for books and staff.

> A special student library committee was formed, and they in turn persuaded a student body of 3000 to assess themselves $10 each toward the library book budget. The result was not only an additional $30,000 for library books, but also convincing and embarrassing evidence to local college officials and the state legislature that more money had to be found for all state university library units. The following year it was found.[4]

One imaginative program, based on a concept tested successfully at Colby College in the 1950s, also involves the entire student body. In this project, a library-student-faculty committee selects a basic list of about six books (classics or contemporary titles) and urges all students to read them. Students can then elect a single title as the following year's "Book of the Year." Teachers in relevant departments might integrate the book into the curriculum. If the author is living, he or she may be invited to the campus. The publisher's representative might also be asked to speak about the work. The library, naturally, becomes a focal point in these programs. Other works by the author may be displayed, and a special bibliography on related subjects may be prepared.

This kind of program is obviously most suited to a small college. Larger institutions, however, have many other opportunities for creative marketing to students. Two notable programs are those of the Robert B. House Undergraduate Library at the University of North Carolina and the Milton S. Eisenhower Library at Johns Hopkins University.

In addition to its faculty newsletter, mentioned above, the Robert B. House library publishes a student newsletter. If there is a story the director feels should also be covered by the student daily newspaper, a call to the editor usually brings a student reporter. (Unlike many student newspapers, the paper at the University of North Carolina will not accept press releases. The paper serves as a training tool for journalists, and the editors believe that the best stories are obtained by having reporters do their own fact-gathering.)

Like many colleges, the University of North Carolina includes a brochure about the library in the orientation packet distributed by the student government. North Carolina, however, does considerably more. All students enrolled in a freshman English program, for example, go to the library during a class period for a formal slide presentation and a tour of the library's facilities. Uses of reference materials, periodicals, search services and special collections are explained. The students are also taught how to use the stacks. (*Playboy Magazine* has singled out the library at the University of North Carolina as "the best place to meet students of the opposite sex." Another interesting way to market the features of an academic library?)

One of the more interesting services of the Robert B. House Library is its Term Paper Consultation Program. Any student preparing a research paper can sign up for a one-on-one session with a reference librarian to discuss the student's project and specific reference needs. A student learns how to prepare his or her own bibliography, how to locate specific periodical citations and, in general, how to take maximum advantage of the resources of the library. The individual clinic serves to build a student's confidence in accomplishing library-related work and to erase the age-old stigma of the library as a stuffy place containing books that nobody can find. Most important, by bringing students and librarians together in the freshman orientation program (which reaches about 90% of all freshmen) or the Term Paper Consultation Program, the library is making its presence felt on campus and convincing students and faculty that it is indispensable.

The Milton S. Eisenhower Library at Johns Hopkins University takes a different approach in marketing its services. In addition to preparing standard descriptive material for the university handbook given to all faculty and students, Susan K. Martin, the library's director, has turned to paid advertising. The library bought a two-page center spread in the student paper to describe the features of the library, outline the many services available and publicize the hours of operation. The Eisenhower Library also sends press releases to the student paper, but the two-page paid spread is far more eye-catching than an editorial column.

Library Director Martin is considering other marketing techniques aimed at students. On the drawing board is a special reception designed for incoming freshmen and new transfer students to meet the members of the library staff and learn about the library's vast resources. Ms. Martin is also considering a self-guided tour of the library in which new students would be given maps containing information about the library's highlights. Numbers on the map would correspond to numbers placed in key areas within the library.

The library currently provides basic library orientation for all freshmen through a student group. Unfortunately, according to Ms. Martin, most freshmen have already visited the library during their initial visits to the university and believe that when they begin school "they know all about the library and what we can offer them." Marketing the academic library to the student body is a most difficult chore when dealing with ambivalence or a know-it-all attitude. Thus, there is an attempt to involve student leaders in the library's marketing campaign through orientation programs involving upperclassmen, the use of the student newspaper and the involvement of student library aids who maintain a positive attitude about the library and its services.

Reaching the Library Staff

A successful marketing effort begins with the library's own staff. According to Eli Oboler, "What should be the most common and important regular publication of any academic library with at least five staff members is a regularly issued—preferably monthly —staff bulletin. It can be an invaluable adjunct to library public relations."[5]

The use of staff newsletters will serve the library in many ways. In a panel discussion at the American Library Association's 1980 annual conference, Sally Brickman, of the Case Western Reserve University Library, identified two basic purposes of the newsletter: It informs the staff of current library happenings, new developments and news directly related to library personnel, and it provides a permanent record of library events and developments. Each issue of her newsletter contains an interview with a library employee, thereby adding a more personal note.

Ms. Brickman, who reports to the library director and acts as an unofficial liaison with the staff, believes the newsletter meets four basic objectives:

• Creates an awareness of the library's goals.

• Keeps the library staff informed of library-related events within the library and outside.

• Increases the effectiveness of staff members, resulting in increased productivity.

• Encourages a favorable staff attitude towards the library as well as fellow staff members.

Joanne R. Euster, director of the San Francisco State Library, has analyzed the role of staff public relations in a way that should be of interest to academic librarians. Ms. Euster defines three basic functions of a staff public relations program: 1) To provide feedback to the library or organization from the staff; 2) To help the organization determine what it must do to obtain the goodwill and cooperation of all members of the staff; 3) To plan and implement means of achieving that goodwill and cooperation.

> People should feel good about their work. However, to do their job well employees need enough information to understand their individual job and also to know how that job fits into the overall job of the library or organization. . . . [Staff public relations] is in part an activity and in part an organizational style and philosophy. The underlying principle to make staff public relations work must be a certain permeability of the organization; a basic assumption that the sharing of information and knowledge is good for the library. This is, in large part, a matter of leadership-style.[6]

To ignore the staff in favor of full concentration on selling the library to patrons and potential benefactors can be a disastrous road to follow. Keeping staff members fully informed and enthusiastic about current and future library developments will assist the director in the overall marketing program.

DISPLAYS AND EXHIBITS

Creating displays and exhibits is an essential element in promoting the academic library. Current topics or celebrations of events such as United Nations Week, the 250th anniversary of Haydn's birth, the centennial of the state, city, school, etc., are ideal opportunities for a display. There are several excellent sources for finding appropriate dates:

A. Black and C. Black, *Writers and Artists Yearbook* (Boston, MA: Writer, Inc., annual).

William D. and Helen M. Chase, comps., *Chases' Calendar of Annual Events* (Flint, MI: Apple Tree Press, annual).

Miriam A. DeFord, *Who Was When?*, 3rd ed. (Bronx, NY: Wilson, 1976).

Linda Millgate, *The Almanac of Dates* (New York: Harcourt Brace Jovanovich, Inc., 1977).

Some examples of displays presented by the Idaho State University Library may be of interest to others in planning:

Tomorrow's Careers
Western Books
That's a No-No! Drugs, Liquor,
    Marijuana and Tobacco
The Defense of America
The Arts in Flux; Art, Drama, Music,
    Film, Television
The End of the Empires
The British Museum and Its Publications
Prehistoric Fauna and Flora
Brazil: A World in Itself
America the Un-Beautiful:
    Why Conservation?

The American University Today
Christ and Revolution
Books from Down Under
America's Black Writers
The Sea: Its Poetry and Practicality
Gems, the Uncommon Stones
Law Enforcement
Japan in the World Picture
New Life for American Cities
Help for Small Business
The Challenge of Crime
100 Years of the Weather Bureau

Staff and Student Resources

In developing a topic for display, it is wise to consult department chairpeople to determine areas that may be of special interest and to solicit materials that may be held by individuals. A professor who has a private collection of books, artifacts, art objects, etc. is usually delighted to lend his collection for a library display. Often special departmental libraries (located apart from the general university library) will contain materials that should be included in a major library exhibit. Museums in various academic departments contain items that should be considered as well.

Naturally, the school's art department should be consulted on topics that involve art or graphics, or for assistance in designing the exhibit. Talented art students may be available as contributors. For example, Sterling Memorial Library, Yale University, takes frequent advantage of its students' artistic output. Drawings or book illustrations created by students are often shown in a display case adjacent to rare book illustrations borrowed from Yale's Beinecke Library (rare book and manuscript collection.) Many libraries use student artists to create posters to advertise and supplement a display.

The technique for planning and undertaking an academic library display will not vary too much from the basic format of planning and carrying out a public library exhibit. There are a few differences, however. The availability of student talent, mentioned above, is one. Also, in most cases, the academic library will have greater resources at its disposal to combine various materials into a fairly elaborate and unified display. Finally, faculty consultation makes it easier to obtain accurate and interesting signs and other informative notices to accompany an exhibit.

Publicizing the Exhibit

Publicity is as important to an exhibit in the academic library as it is in the public library. Many of the techniques described in Chapters 2 and 3 are applicable and should be used to communicate with campus media. If you wish to attract visitors from outside the school, be sure to include local papers and broadcasting stations in your promotion effort. A notice should also appear in the campus weekly calendar. Posters or mimeographed announcements should be placed on the main student bulletin board (usually located in the Student Union), fraternity and sorority houses, dormitories, dining rooms and other campus buildings that provide bulletin board space for general announcements. Posters and announcements should also be displayed in prominent areas in town. Local bookstores, for example, are often eager to cooperate with academic libraries. Consider developing a special format for posters (such as The XYZ Library Presents . . .) to provide a recognition factor.

Whenever possible, a schedule of forthcoming exhibits and displays should be distributed to school and town media. Let the various news outlets have the opportunity to plan to cover your exhibits. You may be requested to provide background information, including pictures, concerning the development of a particular show.

Exhibits and displays serve as attractive, decorative show pieces, as well as educational aids. Most important, they bring people to the library. By preparing a book list or suggested bibliography, the librarian is ready with necessary back-up material for the individual who gets "turned on" by the display and wants to know more. By getting the right book in the hands of the right person, the library is accomplishing one of its primary goals.

ACADEMIC FRIENDS AND ALUMNI GROUPS

Developing good public relations can also be accomplished through an academic Friends of the Library group. Not only do Friends help to promote library events, but they can be most influential in periodic fundraising efforts. According to Eli M. Oboler,

> Perhaps the zenith in American "Friends" groups is the one at Brandeis University, which for many years, through various schemes for raising money, has provided practically all the regular book purchase support for the library there. But this is an unusual, probably unique, situation, not likely to be a national model. Still, it indicates just how far such a group can go if it is dedicated.[7]

Usually, Friends organizations are composed of alumni who try to locate special collections or individual books that are needed by the library but are hard to acquire through regular acquisition channels because of their high cost. Keeping alumni aware of the library's special interests is one way to build the collection. Another is to publicize any major gift of an individual's papers, thereby encouraging other donations.

In soliciting a gift of an individual's papers, be careful not to suggest that the gift may represent a substantial tax savings. While the donation of stocks, bonds, works of art, etc. may have an exact value placed upon them that is acceptable to the Internal Revenue Service, placing a dollar value on personal papers for tax purposes can be difficult. The library should suggest that the gift of manuscripts or personal papers be made with proper legal consultation and accompanied by the necessary legal papers. In addition, certain gifts of private papers are closed for a period of time, at the donor's request, to protect the privacy of the giver or contemporary associates. These various caveats should be clearly spelled out and, of course, observed.

Friends and other academic groups or alumni associations can also be very helpful in fund raising. All college alumni are familiar with the annual letter appealing for funds. Rarely does the library become involved in a direct appeal to alumni for funds. Often a separate appeal by the library can muddy the waters when the various alumni associations are campaigning for the college. Usually, funding for the library from alumni sources should be coordinated with the university's alumni office and not conducted separately.

Alumni-organized book sales have been popular methods of raising money for the library. Perhaps the largest academic book sale is the annual event conducted for the libraries of Brandeis University. The annual sale is held under two large circus tents in a shopping center parking lot in Wilmette, IL. The sale, organized by members of the North Shore Brandeis National Women's Committee, raised nearly $150,000 in May 1981. More than 25,000 book buyers flooded the area, looking for that rare first edition or simply to pick up last year's best sellers for under a dollar. A Hemingway first edition was sold for $3, a complete encyclopedia for $25.

Volunteers prepare for next year's Brandeis sale the day following this year's sale. Books are stored and sorted in a rented warehouse during the year and placed in predetermined aisles well in advance of the first customer's entrance. Maps are printed to assist the bargain hunters find their way among the books. The sale, first held in 1958, attracts people from miles around. One 1981 buyer, Phyllis Erickson of Bettendorf, Iowa, owns her own book store. She acquired 250 books to help boost her store's stock. Said another book sale patron, "This thing's a fixture. You can't walk through the tent without seeing someone you know."[8]

SPECIAL COLLECTIONS

The acquisition of manuscripts, rare books, papers, photographs, etc., is a constant goal of academic libraries. As noted above, Friends' groups can be helpful in acquiring additions to a collection. Sometimes a more elaborate marketing effort is needed, particularly if a collection is of broad scope. A particularly interesting example of a special collection that was made possible by aggressive marketing is the oral history collection at Columbia University, in New York.

The concept originated with Columbia historian Allan Nevins, who in 1948 started to build his own private oral history collection of major figures in the arts, government, sciences, education, business and other areas. Eventually the project became too big for one person. With the aid of funds from the Lucius N. Littauer Foundation, plus full cooperation from the university, an important research center began. Today Columbia's oral history collection is the largest and, perhaps, the most important in the world. Yet no funding came from the general income of the university. Gifts and bequests from individuals, grants from public and private agencies, plus support from the library's Bancroft fund underwrote the project (now the Oral History Research Office, Columbia University).

It took a massive public relations effort to convince foundations, individuals and the university that an oral history collection was a worthwhile undertaking. The promotional campaign was organized by the project's late director, Dr. Louis M. Starr. It received a significant boost when Dr. Starr sold the rights to distribute microform transcripts of the collection to the New York Times Co. Royalties from this arrangement continue to help the project to operate.

Special collections themselves can be viewed as a marketing tool. A major collection will draw researchers from many other institutions and will be publicized in scholarly journals and via word of mouth. The library can benefit greatly from this exposure.

Leading academic libraries have numerous special collections. At Harvard University, for example, the central collection alone (that is, not including library divisions serving primarily the schools of business, divinity, medicine, architecture and others) includes the Hofer Graphic Arts Collection, the Keats Memorial Collection, the Theodore Roosevelt Collection, the Trotsky Archive, and more than 50 author collections ranging from Aristophanes to Thomas Wolfe.

Smaller libraries also have special collections that bring them wide recognition. Many collections reflect the interest of a university department or the history of the region. For example, the libraries at both Haverford and Swarthmore colleges have built extensive book and manuscript collections on the history of the Quaker movement, which has been important in that area of Pennsylvania. Similarly, the William Bennett Bizzell Memorial Library at the University of Oklahoma has developed one of the nation's finest collections devoted to American Indians.

Academic libraries sometimes work with other institutions, particularly state libraries, to develop complementary special collections. To complement the University of Oklahoma's American Indian collection, for example, the state library in Oklahoma City has built upon the university's collection and the Oklahoma State Historical Society has accumulated many unique documents relating to the American Indian. (Its collection of Indian constitutions, for example, is extremely rich.)

One of the nation's finest state historical libraries is the State Historical Society Library in Madison, WI, which has a world-famous collection of materials on labor history and social action groups. Several hundred yards from the State Historical Society Library is the University of Wisconsin–Madison Memorial Library. Rather than develop competing collections, these two superb facilities work in unison to develop collections that supplement each other. Thus, each library's financial resource is used to the maximum extent, and each library builds its own identity.

MAKING MONEY WITH YOUR COLLECTION

Using the library's collection for commercial purposes is being tried more readily by more libraries. Several decades ago a library approached by a commercial publisher with the request to borrow a rare edition almost universally honored the request without question. The reprint book business was built upon the generosity of librarians who felt that their wares were public and should be made available to all who asked and promised the books would not be damaged.

By the mid-1970s, however, library directors realized that their valuable resources were providing healthy profits for the reprint houses with little return to the library. Several of the large university libraries became mass suppliers, first to reprinters, then to micropublishers. Under the guidance of Eugene Powers, a brilliant business leader and library benefactor, University Microfilms, Inc. was founded in Ann Arbor, MI. It was not a coincidence that the University of Michigan's University Library was located in the same city. For years, the University of Michigan Libraries supplied many of the materials that were committed to microform and sold to other libraries throughout the world.

When library directors understood that their wares were serving a commercial purpose with little return to the library, lending policies began to change. Whereas a scholar could borrow material without charge, a commercial firm that wished to use material either to reprint or commit to microform was charged a fee of approximately $25 per volume. The firm was required to return the material either re-bound or in the same condition it was in when it left the library. Many libraries also requested a complimentary copy of the publisher's edition.

The next step in developing a working relationship with publishing concerns was to enter into contractual arrangements involving fees, royalties and advances against royalties. A library with a unique collection learned that micropublishers were glad to film the collection at the publisher's expense, pay the library a royalty or fee, and supply a microform edition to the library. Thus, original, rare and often fragile manuscripts and documents could be kept in an archival chamber while scholars used the microform editions for their research. This arrangement served to improve the library's income but also served to enhance the importance of the library's collection as more and more people learned of its existence. Another, perhaps more valuable purpose was also accomplished. Many libraries had important collections of rare periodicals with some issues missing. The micropublisher was able to locate the missing pieces at other university libraries, film them and provide a complete edition of a single title.

One of the most ambitious undertakings involved a small, but highly successful micropublisher, Research Publications, Inc. (Woodbridge, CT), and two of the world's finest business libraries: the Goldsmith Library at the London School of Economics and the Kress Library at Harvard University's Graduate School of Business Administration. By combining both collections a unique microform library of business and management was published. The result is probably the best collection of historic business materials ever assembled. Both libraries share in royalty payments and both have profited substantially from sales.

Not all libraries have a collection that justifies a commercial micropublisher's effort and investment. For the library that believes it has a unique collection it would pay to write to several major micropublishers (see *Guide to Microforms in Print,* published annually by Microform Review, for listings) and describe the collection. A micropublisher will need to have a description of the collection, rough number of pages, format of the collection (i.e., books, manuscripts, letters, newspapers, etc.), physical size of the material, and an estimate of the condition. If a micropublisher is interested, he will either request that you send your collection to his laboratory for filming and processing or, if this is not possible, make arrangements to film on site. Since the cost of on-site filming is considerably higher, a publisher may be discouraged if you insist that material cannot leave the library.

If a micropublisher agrees to film your material, the library usually receives a royalty ranging from 8% to 15% of publisher's net receipts. In addition, the library should receive a complimentary copy of the film. Naturally, material borrowed from the library must be returned in good condition. Often old volumes will require rebinding after filming. This is done at the micropublisher's expense.

MARKETING SPECIAL SERVICES

Marketing special services can present problems if the staff is unfamiliar with the service or if there is not a well-orchestrated promotional campaign. The rapid growth of technology in the library requires particular attention. Automated circulation systems, electronic security systems, computer-based catalogs and online information retrieval services are becoming commonplace in libraries, particularly in academic settings. Both staff and patrons must be educated about the features and value of these devices. There is little doubt that technological innovations are turning the library of the future into the library of today. A library that fails to comprehend and communicate the importance of automated services may well find itself the library of the past.

According to Alice H. Bahr, project librarian/government publications at the Muhlenberg College Library, "The reluctance of some librarians to actively promote online services reflects a healthy concern that staff might be inundated with more work than it can handle, but it also reflects an unwillingness to accept the fact that such services redefine the nature of reference work."[9] This comment underlines the need to promote new services to staff as well as patrons, particularly when the service involves what many consider complicated electronic equipment.

Thus, the initial step in marketing a special service is to acquaint the staff fully with the system, its potentials and possible pitfalls. "There is little likelihood that promotional materials and activities will reflect system capability if staff members aren't given sufficient time to exploit the system. To allow staff to become comfortable with equipment, most libraries use a system a few weeks or months before publicizing it."[10] The Computer Based Information Center Staff at Philadelphia's Free Library spent three months working with the New York Times Information Bank before announcing the service's availability. The staff at Lehigh University's library spent a month testing its online equipment before promoting it.

Marketing special services to patrons uses the same basic techniques as for other library services. Posters, press releases, special displays and group meetings all serve to inform the public. Fortunately, some vendors of specialized services or equipment supply free materials for promotional purposes. Major vendors of online services (Lockheed, SDC Search Service and BRS) will supply libraries with posters or other promotional pieces, including ads, to assist in a marketing campaign. Many of the vendors of online services also allow libraries a reduced connect rate when the libraries are providing demonstrations to students, faculty and fellow librarians. By promoting a special service, such as the online service, many librarians have discovered that patrons become aware of other library services as well.

PROMOTING THE SPECIAL LIBRARY

Marketing the special library, particularly in a corporate setting, often requires a different set of guidelines. Rarely, for example, does the library serve the public as, to a limited extent, do most academic libraries. In fact, many special libraries make it a policy to deny the public access to staff or materials. By its very definition, the special library is designed to provide maximum service to the specific audience that has created the library and, in most cases, pays the bills. Marketing to this audience becomes much easier when it is possible to define, almost to the individual, who will be using the library's services.

Elizabeth Ferguson, former librarian of the Institute of Life Insurance, lists promotion among the basic functions of an outstanding special library:

1. The library provides the material for essential research in the conduct of a business.

2. The library provides reference service to assist in essential research.

3. The library *promotes its services* so that employees look to it for assistance.[11] (Italics added.)

Ms. Ferguson also writes: "It is not surprising that one often hears special librarians say that their major problem is to 'educate management.' I submit, however, that there is a most unattractive air of superiority in this phrase, and I would like to see it eliminated from our public relations vocabulary. *Inform, interpret*—yes—but not *educate*."[12]

Special libraries vary widely in size and services. Many are very small, staffed by a single librarian with perhaps a clerical assistant. Others have hundreds of thousands of volumes in their collections and comparably larger staffs. Some large companies with multiple locations have separate libraries, or "information centers," as they are increasingly being called, in different facilities. Usually these satellite libraries specialize in the particular area of research at that facility. A Union catalog usually unites the corporate collection.

In most corporate libraries, the library director is responsible for the development and implementation of a library marketing program. Funds are generally taken from the overall library budget. The library director may report directly to top management or to a department head, such as the chief of administrative services, research and development, public information, or information systems, if the library is a unit of that department.

Whatever its size and place within the organization, the special library must begin its marketing effort by informing all potential users of the library's existence, its location, its telephone number(s), and an overview of the many services offered that will save both time and money. Many corporations include a discussion of library services during the period of new employee orientation. Some organizations provide printed handouts containing pertinent information about the library. Unfortunately, since the new employee is also burdened with handouts from every other company service ranging from insurance and retirement benefits to profit sharing and stock options, it is more than likely that the library's brochure will receive too little attention. It becomes necessary, therefore, for the special library to develop an ongoing and continuous program to inform its patrons of its services.

Examples of Corporate Library Marketing

McGraw-Hill, Inc., a company with several corporate information centers serving its various divisions, has a fine central library that distributes a monthly bibliography of recently received materials to key corporate personnel. The bibliographic listing is organized by subject and contains titles of both books and periodicals. Executives who are interested in receiving one or more of the listed titles simply check off the name(s) and return the bibliography to the library; the requested material is then forwarded to them. Noncirculating reference material is starred on the bibliography and is available for use only within the library. The system keeps employees aware of the library's continuing effort to acquire current material and also assures employees that they will be kept abreast of important professional developments.

At Exxon, the information center is part of the company's administrative service division. The manager of administrative service reports directly to the corporation's secretary. Thus, the information center is highly visible from the top of the corporate ladder. Like many other large corporate libraries, Exxon's information center provides all company employees with a publication (published semimonthly) that details current library-related developments. A video tape explaining library services is available to all employees and is shown to all new employees. A separate brochure explaining the center's available data bases is also produced. The director of Exxon's information center, Mary Rizzo, is responsible for public relations.

At the Seattle–First National Bank, the manager of the library is a corporate assistant vice president, Jeannette Privat. She believes that special librarians should "quit talking to ourselves and begin talking to others." Ms. Privat has elevated her library to an essential element in the bank's operations. To communicate with management, the library publishes a quarterly report on departmental operations. In addition, the library produces an annual usage questionnaire for major departmental users. (See Figure 6.2.) This enables the library to get some feedback on the quality of its services, to obtain information on user plans for the coming year, and to remind users that "they are getting a lot of service from the library."

Other promotional activities include a "How to Use the Library" talk at departmental and branch staff meetings; presentations at regional managers' meetings; slide-tape presentations at branch staff meetings; a section in the bank's "Business Service Package Operating Guide" on methods of obtaining information for officer calls; and announcements and articles in the bank's newsletter and magazine. Library services are mentioned in new employee orientation programs, and individual tours are given to new employees, particularly officers and researchers.

At the General Foods Marketing Information Center, manager Lois Seulowitz begins her "selling" program by providing new employees with a brochure listing samples of typical questions the information center is prepared to handle. As part of the general orientation for new employees, a film strip explains the information center and its many services. Articles on recent technical developments related to General Foods' operations, along with current bibliographic information, appear in the company's newspaper and in appropriate corporate bulletins aimed at a specific audience. When a new periodical is received by the information center, the table of contents is photocopied and distributed to approximately 700 employees who have asked to receive information in their special field of interest. Visitors or employees passing through the General Foods lobby can see an attractive display describing the information center and the various ways it is being used. (At General Foods, the public can use the company information center by appointment.)

Bell Telephone Laboratories Inc. has developed a networking information resource that is being shared by the company's 22 libraries. Eight separate computer systems now can access more than 200 data bases around the country. "The image we had in mind when we decided to pool our resources was a library without walls," says Robert A. Kennedy, director of Bell Labs' libraries and information center. Marketing the features and advantages of this vast resource is accomplished through articles in company newsletters, descriptive brochures and individual demonstrations.

A Special Library in a Not-for-Profit Agency

There are, of course, many special libraries that are not part of profit-making organizations. They include libraries at foundations, museums, research institutes, associations, unions, etc. Nina Root, director of the library of the American Museum of Natural History, believes that the best way to show the importance and strength of her library to the individuals responsible for its support is to maintain a high degree of visibility. "I am very active in many professional organizations and I encourage other members of our library staff to be active as well." Ms. Root writes articles for both library and museum publications, thereby keeping her library and the museum in the spotlight.

The library uses various other marketing techniques. In October 1981, for example, Ms. Root organized a conference in Philadelphia on the "Bibliography of Natural History." Attendees included librarians from U.S. and foreign museums, as well as scientists interested in learning about research tools available to them. The library also produces a column, "Recent Publications in Natural History," which is published in the museum's regular publication, *Curator*. The bibliography contains full citations for new materials organized into 12 separate categories. In addition, the library selects at least one major new title and obtains a detailed review from one of the museum's curators for publication in *Curator*.

Since the museum's library is also open to the public, the library maintains a permanent display case in the public viewing area. Called Library Gallery, the case often shows rare books from the library's extensive collection or photographs taken by explorers or naturalists that may never have been previously exhibited. The library has a policy, shared by many other not-for-profit special libraries, of lending material to other libraries or organizations for display. Thus, artifacts from the museum's library can serve as "public relations representatives" when they are on loan.

MARKETING TIPS FOR THE SPECIAL LIBRARIAN

In order to provide good services and, in turn, to promote them, special librarians must above all keep abreast of developments in their patrons' area of interest. Often this requires reading technical literature, taking special courses (usually reimbursed by the company or organization), attending meetings and briefing sessions and becoming familiar with the organization's business. If the librarian is not interested in electronics then he or she will have a serious problem marketing the services of a library serving a company in the electronics field. "A sharp librarian can make as good a vice-president as can a sharp salesman moved up from the ranks, but he must know more than how to classify and arrange information. He needs to be indispensable to the company and to thoroughly understand management, planning, operations research, the company's special field *and* public relations."[13]

Dr. Herbert White, dean of the Indiana University Graduate Library School and former president of the Special Libraries Association, comments:

> Libraries must recognize that the organization has its own needs and the successful library will develop its plans to satisfy those needs. Developing relationships with individuals who, in turn, will broadcast the library's value and importance is but one way to improve the library's image. Too often, libraries have tried to serve the needs of all segments of the corporate or public community and, as a result, have failed to serve any of the needs successfully. The successful library is an aggressive library. It will search out and locate its clientele, then state: "It's my job to help you. What are your problems?" Perhaps Donald Urquhardt (former director, British National Lending Library) said it best: "McDonalds did not get rich selling hamburgers to vegetarians."[14]

Figure 6.2   Seattle–First National Bank's Library Usage Questionnaire

INTER-OFFICE CORRESPONDENCE

To _____   *From* Jeannette Privat
_____

_____   Assistant Vice President & Manager
                                         Library
_____   HOB -12

Subject ___ *Library Usage* _____   *Phone* __4056__
                                                            Date __10/14/80__

During the last year, your area was a frequent user of Library services. To help us meet your future needs, we would appreciate your taking a few minutes to answer the attached questions which pertain to your expected usage in 1981.

If possible, we would like to have the questionnaire returned by October 22nd. Thank you for your assistance.

**Library Usage
Questionnaire**

Please check the appropriate boxes which pertain to your expected level of usage in 1981. For reference, your approximate level of usage in 1980 is listed in the second column.

Service	Your Area's Approximate Level of Usage in 1980*	Expected Level of Usage of This Service in 1981				
		Much Higher	Higher	Same	Lower	Much Lower
Research Services		☐	☐	☐	☐	☐
Ordering Publications		☐	☐	☐	☐	☐
Routing Periodicals		☐	☐	☐	☐	☐
Renewing Subscriptions		☐	☐	☐	☐	☐
Photocopying Articles,		☐	☐	☐	☐	☐

Comments:

_____

*Because of the record-keeping expense, we don't keep complete statistics but have approximated the usage. Numbers are based on 9 months of actual data.

Figure 6.2   (Cont.)

Additionally, to help us serve you better, we would appreciate your answering the following questions concerning the quality of our existing services.

	Very Good	**Good**	**Needs Improvement***
Research Services	☐	☐	☐
Comments:			
Ordering Publications	☐	☐	☐
Comments:			
Routing Publications	☐	☐	☐
Comments:			
Renewing Subscriptions	☐	☐	☐
Comments:			
Photocopying Articles,	☐	☐	☐
Comments:			

Thank you for your responses. Please return the questionnaire to:

Jeannette Privat
Library
HOB - 12

*If you have checked "needs improvement" in any area, please indicate in the comments section what aspect concerns you.

_____

Source: Seattle–First National Bank. Reprinted with permission.

Marketing special libraries means keeping a constant lookout for another way to get the message across. If the organization publishes a newsletter or company paper, the librarian should talk with the editor and request a special column for library news or suggest the use of fillers prepared by and attributed to the library. If the organization is involved in an acquisition, the library is a natural source of information about the acquiring or acquired company. A well-written, interesting article will inform all company personnel and also show that the library is in the forefront of news and information gathering. The library can organize a regular book review column on works of particular interest to personnel. Facts and figures concerning the corporation can be sent regularly to certain managers, e.g., those responsible for stockholder relations.

A few large corporations have an external house organ. The library can help the editor as well as itself by suggesting stories or supplying information on a regular basis. A memo to the corporate public relations department suggesting a series of articles on the history of the organization or on the special field in which the organization is involved will undoubtedly mean the library will be called upon to assist in locating information, photographs, etc.

Some companies are particularly interested in preserving and promoting their history. Companies that maintain extensive corporate archives should work directly with the library. An aggressive librarian might suggest that the history-minded company take a few steps beyond maintaining files. Should select corporate material be preserved on microfilm? If so, the librarian should become involved in the selection and indexing process.

How about oral histories? Many corporations have already started an oral history collection covering both company history and the development of a specific industry. For example, Federated Department Stores has an extensive collection covering company policies, methods, changes in consumer tastes and buying habits, etc. The Weyerhaeuser Timber Company has developed an oral history program detailing lumbering practices, labor problems, immigration and corporate developments involving Weyerhaeuser as well as many of its competing firms. The special librarian should become involved in this kind of information-gathering program.

Suggesting new programs to management shows the library as a vital, active part of the organization and not simply an information storeroom. If management is favorably impressed with the suggestions offered by the special librarian, it is likely that a request will be made for a more detailed action plan complete with budgetary projections. Thus, the librarian becomes involved in basic management techniques. Most important, by promoting the special library to those individuals who are responsible for its future, the librarian serves the interests of the parent organization and also assures that the library will not be ignored during budget time or periods of general business unrest.

A final word on marketing the special library and one that is applicable to all library promotion efforts: Word of mouth is often the best public relations tool. Find that elusive fact or citation for a patron once, and you can be sure that a positive image of the library will result. Or, as Holgar J. Johnson, former president of the Institute of Life Insurance put it, public relations is "90% doing a good job and only 10% telling about it, important though that is."[15]

FOOTNOTES

1. George S. Bobinski, "Case Studies in Library Public Relations," *Kentucky Library Association Bulletin* 34 (April 1970): 16.

2. Laurence Miller, "Liaison Work in the Academic Library," *RQ* 16 (Spring 1977): 213.

3. Ibid., p. 215.

4. Bobinski, op. cit., p. 13.

5. Eli M. Oboler, "Selling the Academic Library," in *Public Relations for Libraries,* ed. Allan Angoff (Westport, CT: Greenwood Press, 1973), p. 147.

6. Joanne R. Euster, "Staff Public Relations is Not a Newsletter" (Paper delivered at the American Library Association Annual Conference, July 1, 1980).

7. Oboler, op. cit., p. 142.

8. *The New York Times,* June 1, 1981, p. 7.

9. Alice H. Bahr, "Promotion of Online Services," in *The Library and Information Manager's Guide to Online Services,* ed. Ryan E. Hoover (White Plains, NY: Knowledge Industry Publications, Inc., 1980), p. 161.

10. Bahr, op. cit., p. 163.

11. Elizabeth Ferguson, "Creation and Development of an Insurance Library," in *Public Relations for Libraries,* ed. Allan Angoff (Westport, CT: Greenwood Press, 1973), p. 188.

12. Ibid.

13. Josephine Raburn, "Public Relations for a 'Special' Public," *Special Libraries* (December 1969): 650.

14. Telephone interview with author.

15. Ferguson, op. cit., p. 182.

7

Summary and Conclusions

We take the library for granted. It was here when we were growing up; it will be here when our grandchildren grow up. But will it? There is little doubt that the national trend toward budget cutting and the trimming of public services will continue to have an adverse impact on libraries. Already, some public libraries have had to cut staff, reduce services and, in some instances, close branches. Academic and special libraries, too, must fight for support as their budgets are eroded by steadily increasing costs.

The problem has not been ignored by librarians, who have vigorously pleaded their cause through professional conferences, as well as by newsletters and personal appeals to local, state and national decision makers. Such appeals are important, but they are not enough. The *users* of the library must be persuaded to join the battle to help the library. In the case of the public library, this means the members of the community—the voters— whose influence on public officials is far greater than that of an individual library director. In the case of the academic library, it means both faculty and students, to whom library services should be among the most important resources of their institutions. For the corporate library, it means all employees who rely on quickly available, accurate information to do their jobs well.

Librarians must reach out to both current and potential patrons and convince them that library services are essential. To do so effectively, they must understand, and apply, some basic principles of marketing.

To many, marketing is a dirty word. It prompts visions of selling soap or used cars. This philosophy, if related to the selling of a library's services, will have disastrous results. In most cases, the patron who receives a newsletter or announcement of a new service doesn't consider the library as a huckster but as a purveyor of information. And the dissemination of information is, of course, a primary function of the library.

113

ASPECTS OF LIBRARY MARKETING

To convey the message does not require an expensive public relations consultant or massive advertising campaign. Rather, it can be a simple matter of doing what the library does best—informing. People should assume that the library is the source of first resort when a question occurs that can't be answered through home reference books. Students should know that the public library (and, in some instances, the library at a local college or business) is a valuable resource when material is not available in the school library.

Use the Media

A relationship with the media is crucial to a library's marketing effort. Such a relationship is not difficult to establish. Both newspapers and local radio and TV stations are looking for news. News is their business. The library can help the media do their job and, at the same time, sell the services of the library, by working cooperatively with the press. A news release doesn't have to carry an earth shattering message. It simply has to provide information of value to the readers, viewers or listeners. Obviously, a value judgment must be made as to the relative importance of the "news." However, with an understanding of the needs and interests of the audience, the library director or public relations specialist can easily provide appropriate material.

A library newsletter conveys the latest information concerning new books and services and also keeps the library in the public eye. Corporations spend millions of dollars a year keeping their names before the public, even if they do not sell a product or service directly to the consumer. It's pretty hard to buy a product from Boeing, but most people know the name. The library, too, must keep its name before the public.

Another important source of library information is the annual report. The report, usually prepared by the library's director, provides details of the previous year's activities, including statistical data. The report is usually given to the officials responsible for library operations and should also be made available to the general public. Ways to disseminate the report range from placing an ample supply at the circulation desk to a community-wide mailing.

Offer Special Events

It is also important for the library to offer a varied array of exhibits, displays and programs. Such activities serve the interests of the public and are another way to promote community recognition of the library's value. Creative displays, exhibits, book fairs and programs (speakers, musical events, films, plays, etc.) bring people to the library. The aim is to make the library as important an element in an individual's or family's lifestyle as the television set or local movie theater.

Moreover, the person who comes to the library to view an exhibit of, for example, popular sheet music may come back to borrow a book on the history of the American musical theater—especially if the library has prepared a bibliography or reading list to accompany the exhibit. Thus a special program becomes not only educational and/or entertaining in itself, but it can increase the use of what is still the library's greatest intellectual and recreational resource: books.

Keep in Touch with Community Leaders

Marketing the library involves a liaison with local political and civic groups. Communication starts by simply picking up the telephone or writing a letter and is maintained through ongoing effort. A strong, working Friends group can be a tremendous asset in maintaining community relations. It is particularly important to keep in touch with the individuals who control the library's financial future. To do otherwise is suicide.

Be a Fund Raiser

Fund raising is a special art that often seems to demand professional public relations skills. Librarians can, however, do their own fund raising, particularly if they work with a Friends organization. In fact, in many cases librarians make the best fund raisers because they can understand and communicate the library's needs in a way that outsiders cannot. Government, corporate and foundation grants may be sought for major projects, but individual donors from the community are the likeliest sources of funds. Fund raising should be an ongoing activity, and the library should maintain a want list of needed items at all times.

Nonpublic Libraries

Marketing techniques for the nonpublic library are similar to those for the public library. Academic librarians must make sure that faculty, students and, of course, the administration are kept abreast of library activities. A corporate library director must make sure that management is aware of the services the library is providing, lest the corporate library wind up at the bottom of the heap when budgets are allocated.

SOURCES OF FURTHER INFORMATION

It is hoped that this book has provided some guidance to librarians who have had little previous experience with marketing and who find themselves in the unexpected position of "public relations specialist" or "fund raiser." More information is available from the Library Public Relations Council, Suite 1242, 60 E. 42 St., New York, NY 10017. A few helpful newsletters are *Library PR News* (PO Box 687, Bloomfield, NJ 07003) and *Unabashed Librarian* (GPO Box 2673, New York, NY 10001). The publications listed in the Bibliography are other sources of information.

WHY MARKET THE LIBRARY?

The future holds little hope that the cost of books, periodicals and other library materials will go down or even stabilize. Rarely, during the past few years, has a library's budget increased at a rate to match the accelerated cost of items to be purchased. Nor have budgets kept pace with operating expenses—salaries (low though they are), building maintenance, supplies, postage, etc. The result is fewer books and materials for the library and fewer opportunities for the library to serve the public that pays the bills.

It is essential that librarians use all the tools at their disposal to convey their message to their audience. The library—be it public, academic or corporate—is an essential element in the bloodstream of the community it serves. To curtail the services of the library is counter-productive to the needs of an open society. The librarian as well as the public at large must assume a fair share of the burden to assure that the library system not just survives but is strengthened.

Bibliography

Angoff, Allan, ed. *Public Relations for Libraries*. Westport, CT: Greenwood Press, 1973.

Bahr, Alice Harrison. "Promotion of Online Services." In *The Library and Information Manager's Guide to Online Services*, edited by Ryan E. Hoover. White Plains, NY: Knowledge Industry Publications, Inc., 1980.

Barber, Peggy. "Library Public Relations." In *ALA Yearbook: 1977*. Chicago, IL: American Library Association, 1977.

Berry, John. "The 'Marketization' of Libraries." *Library Journal*, January 1, 1981, p. 5.

Bobinski, George S. "Case Studies in Library Public Relations." *Kentucky Library Association Bulletin* 34 (1970): 13-16.

Boorstin, Daniel J. *Gresham's Law: Knowledge or Information?* Washington, DC: Library of Congress, 1980.

Boss, Richard W. *Grant Money & How To Get It: A Handbook for Librarians*. New York: R.R. Bowker Co., 1980.

Bowker Annual of Library & Book Trade Information. New York: R.R. Bowker Co., 1980.

Chazeau, M.G. de. "The Cornell Public Library and its Friends." *Wilson Library Bulletin* 31 (1957): 517-20.

Edinger, Joyce. "Marketing Library Services: Strategy for Survival." *College & Research Libraries*, July 1980, pp. 328-32.

Garvey, Mona. *Library Public Relations: A Practical Handbook*. New York: H.W. Wilson Co., 1980.

Harris, W. Best. "Public Relations for Public Libraries." *Assistant Librarian* 64 (1971): 18-19.

Hoey, P. "Public Relations: The Soft Sell." *Aslib Proceedings* 25 (1973): 375-80.

Holtzman, Elizabeth. "Libraries and the Federal Scene." *Bookmark*, Fall 1979, p. 264.

Jackson, A. "Publicity: or, Selling the Information Service." *Aslib Proceedings* 25 (1973): 385-89.

Kies, Cosette. *Projecting A Positive Image Through Public Relations*. Chicago, IL: American Library Association, 1978.

Kohn, Rita, and Tepper, Krysta. *You Can Do It: A PR Skills Manual for Librarians*. Metuchen, NJ: Scarecrow Press, 1981.

Kotler, Philip. *Marketing for Nonprofit Organizations*. Englewood Cliffs, NJ: Prentice-Hall, 1975.

Lesly, Philip. *Lesly's Public Relations Handbook*. Englewood Cliffs, NJ: Prentice-Hall, 1971.

Loizeaux, Marie D. *Publicity Primer*. New York: H.W. Wilson Co., 1959.

Marchant, M. "Public Relations and Library Power." *Idaho Librarian* 25 (1973): 100-106.

Miller, Laurence. "Liaison Work in the Academic Library." *RQ* 16 (1977): 213-15.

The New York Times, June 1, 1981, p. 7.

Norton, Alice. "Why Does a Public Library Need Public Relations?" *Catholic Library World* 48 (1977): 289-91.

O'Donnell, P. "Ways in Which Librarians Can Inform the Public About Services and Resources." *Wyoming Library Roundup* 28 (1973): 31-38.

Oboler, Eli. "Public Relations and Intellectual Freedom." *Pacific Northwest Library Association Quarterly* 38 (1974): 17-21.

Posner, Marcia. "P.P. & P.R. Two Keys to Circulation Success." *SLJ School Library Journal* 22 (1976): 15.

Practical Public Relations. Columbus, OH: Ohio Educational Library/Media Association, 1979.

"Prepare: The Library Public Relations Recipe Book." Preconference publication of the Public Relations Section, Library Administration Division, American Library Association, 1978. Mimeographed.

Price, Derek J. de Solla. *Little Science, Big Science.* New York: Columbia University Press, 1963.

The Public Papers of the Presidents of the United States, 1961-1963. Washington, DC: U.S. Government Printing Office, 1964.

"Publicizing Library Service to Business." *RQ* 16 (1977): 213-15.

"Putting the Library on a Computer." *Business Week,* March 30, 1981, pp. 104-106.

Raburn, Josephine. "Public Relations for a 'Special' Public." *Special Libraries,* December 1969, p. 650.

Rice, Betty. "Programming—the Way and the Worth of It." *Pennsylvania Library Association Bulletin* 31 (1976): 126-28.

_____. *Public Relations for Public Libraries.* New York: H.W. Wilson Co., 1972.

Sherman, Steve. *The ABC's of Library Promotion.* Metuchen, NJ: Scarecrow Press, 1980.

Swan, J. "New Visibility for the Small Library." *Wilson Library Bulletin* 51 (1977): 424-29.

Wallace, Sarah Leslie. *Friends of the Library.* Chicago, IL: American Library Association, 1962.

_____. *Promotion Ideas for Public Libraries.* Chicago, IL: American Library Association, 1953.

Wedgeworth, Robert, ed. *ALA World Encyclopedia of Library and Information Services.* Chicago, IL: American Library Association, 1980.

Index

ABOUT THE AUTHOR

Benedict A. Leerburger is president of the Board of Trustees, Scarsdale (NY) Public Library and a member of the Board of Directors of the Westchester (County) Library System. He is the author of *Josiah Willard Gibbs, American Theoretical Physicist* and editor of *Cowles Encyclopedia of Science, Industry & Technology.* His articles have appeared in many consumer and trade magazines. A freelance writer and editor, Mr. Leerburger previously held numerous editorial positions, including editor in chief of McGraw-Hill Book Co.'s Webster/McGraw-Hill Division, editorial director of KTO Press and managing editor of the Book Division of *Look* magazine. He is a graduate of Colby College.